SURVEY OF OBJECTIVE STUDIES OF PSYCHOANALYTIC CONCEPTS

A Report Prepared for the Committee on Social Adjustment

BY

ROBERT R. SEARS

Professor of Child Psychology
Child Welfare Research Station
State University of Iowa

GREENWOOD PRESS, PUBLISHERS
WESTPORT, CONNECTICUT

Library of Congress Cataloging in Publication Data

Sears, Robert Richardson, 1908-
    Survey of objective studies of psychanalytic
concepts.

    Reprint of the 1943 ed. published by the Social
Science Researh Council, New York, which was issued
as its Bulletin 51.
    Bibliography: p.
    Includes index.
    1. Psychoanalysis.   I. Social Science Research
Council.   Committee on Social Adjustment.   II.   Ti-
tle.   III.   Series: Social Science Research Council
Bulletin ; 51.
[BF173.S44   1979]   150'.19'52   79-4476
ISBN 0-313-21249-X

Published in 1943 by the Social Science Research Council,
New York

Reprinted in 1979 by Greenwood Press, Inc.
51 Riverside Avenue, Westport, CT 06880

Printed in the United States of America

10 9 8 7 6 5 4 3 2 1

The Social Science Research Council was organized in 1923 and formally incorporated in 1924, composed of representatives chosen from the seven constituent societies and from time to time from related disciplines such as law, geography, psychiatry, medicine, and others. It is the purpose of the Council to plan, foster, promote, and develop research in the social field.

2073701

CONSTITUENT ORGANIZATIONS

American Anthropological Association

American Economic Association

American Historical Association

American Political Science Association

American Psychological Association

American Sociological Society

American Statistical Association

v

FOREWORD

No ONE OF THE Social Sciences has escaped the impact of the concepts and technics that are included within the term Psychoanalysis. These have been variously employed in the interpretation of normal and abnormal behavior of individuals and of groupings of individuals. Persons and epochs in history, crime and delinquency, labor problems and the processes of education and reeducation have been analyzed in psychoanalytic terms. Many workers in the fields of the social sciences would accept the statement that "Freud made the greatest contributions of our times to the study of man in relation to himself and others," and would find in psychoanalytic doctrines the key to all social adjustment.

These concepts and technics originated in the clinical treatment of certain types of patients, whereas in one form or another, their use has been gradually extended in ever widening circles without the systematic checking to which scientific concepts are necessarily subjected. It seemed to the Subcommittee on Motivation of the Social Science Research Council's Committee on Social Adjustment that a useful purpose would be served by the preparation of a report on the scientific status of Freudian concepts. The report (1) should discuss the studies which have sought scientific verification of certain of the psychoanalytic concepts, and (2) should suggest programs for research on others which have not yet been thus tested.

Dr. Sears was engaged to perform this twofold service. To keep the assignments within reasonable scope, he was requested to limit his review primarily (1) to concepts rather than technics, and (2) to those concepts which are recognized as Freudian, neglecting the many variants of these which have emanated from his successors and from competing schools of thought. This report has been accepted, and is being published, in the belief that it has significance and potential usefulness.

A. T. POFFENBERGER

PREFACE

HALF A CENTURY AGO, when Freud began to formulate his theories, experimental psychologists could offer him little help. Their natural preoccupation with the methodology of the young science had led to the investigation of problems in which the variables could be clearly defined and precisely measured. The kinds of behavior with which Freud dealt did not at that time seem possible of accurate investigation by these methods. Freud, concerned with the practical problem of healing, could not wait for the slow development of experimental techniques, and proceeded to the construction of a theory of personality with the clinical techniques available to him. This independent growth of psychoanalysis and experimental psychology inevitably led to differences in the kinds of concepts evolved and the systematic structures erected with them.

In recent years, however, rapid strides have been made in the development of objective techniques for studying the kinds of behavior to which Freud applied himself. This, together with the practical desirability of dealing with such problems, has led to a healthy growth of interest in Freud's writings on the part of students trained in the experimental tradition. They have sought to resystematize psychoanalytic concepts and principles in terms of current academic psychologies, and have, in a good number of cases, tried to subject these notions to investigation by other than psychoanalytic methods. In some instances Freud's views have been supported and his principles importantly extended. In others, the new techniques have failed to cast much useful light on the behavior in question. All the work, however, serves to emphasize the increasing significance attached to psychoanalysis, by non-analysts, as a guide to the planning of research on personality.

The present report is a summary and appraisal of published investigations, both experimental and observational, that relate to problems and concepts deriving from Freudian theory. Unhappily there has been no simple way of deciding what materials to include. So much of the psychology of personality is an outgrowth of psychoanalysis that, in a sense, everything about personality is relevant. But in order to keep the report of reasonable length, only those data have been included that relate to Freud's own theoretical formulations. This policy has not been as inhibiting as it might seem, for, with the exception of a very small group of recent dissidents, no other analyst has made a major theoretical contribution; and the reexamination of orthodox concepts by such analysts as Horney and Kardiner is too recent to have influenced the collection of data.

A further selection has been made within Freud's own theory. The material relating to aggression has been excluded because Freud never formalized his theories of aggression or the death instinct in such a way as to make the experimental data particularly relevant. The concept of substitution is almost equally vague, and the experimental data that relate to it, mostly from Lewin's laboratories, deal with a kind of behavior so radically different from that to which Freud applied the concept that little would be gained from an evaluation of it. A few studies have been made of the psychoanalytic process itself, but since none of these was designed to test any theoretical point, they have also been excluded. A summary of these studies, as well as of the experimental literature on both aggression and substitution, is being published elsewhere (Sears, 1943).

A word must be said as to the quality of the data available for consideration in this survey. Much of the observational material quoted was secured by investigators whose interests had nothing to do with psychoanalysis. Their studies concerned other matters altogether, and some of them may be astonished to find their data put to the present use. Such material has been included in order to secure as complete a bibliography of relevant studies as possible.

In its final stages, the entire manuscript was read by Professors L. S. Cottrell, Jr., R. Linton, H. A. Murray, Jr., A. T. Poffenberger, E. B. Wilson, and R. S. Woodworth. To them goes the writer's earnest appreciation for their many helpful suggestions, happy correctives, and provocative criticisms.

October 1942   *Robert R. Sears*

CONTENTS

I. EROTOGENESIS   1
  Oral erotism   2
    1. Thumbsucking   2
    2. Nailbiting   9
    3. Oral gestures   11
  Anal erotism   14
  Genital erotism   15
  The erotogenic complex   18
    1. Oral components   19
    2. Simultaneous stimulation   20
  Conclusions   21
II. EROTIC BEHAVIOR OF CHILDREN   23
  Pregenital sexuality   23
  Genital sexuality   28
    1. Sex play   28
    2. Sex curiosity   29
    3. Overstimulation and sexual aggressions   32
  Conclusions   36
III. OBJECT CHOICE   38
  The self as object   39
    1. Narcissism   39
    2. Masturbation   40
  The Oedipus situation   41
    1. Parent preferences   42
    2. Other heterosexual cathexes   43
  Latency period   45
  Homosexuality   47
    1. Oedipus influence   47
    2. Hamilton's syndrome   49
    3. Associative homosexuality   51
  The marital partner   54
  Experimental control of cathexis   55
  Conclusions   57

IV. DISTORTIONS OF SEXUALITY 59
  Hyposexuality 59
    1. Orgasm inadequacy 59
    2. Lack of sex drive 62
  Hypersexuality and perversion 62
  The anal character 67
  Sublimation 70
  Paranoia 71
  Conclusions 74
V. FIXATION AND REGRESSION 76
  Object fixation 78
    1. Development of object fixations 78
    2. Strength of fixation 79
    3. Interference effect of object fixations 80
  Instrumental act fixation 81
    1. Amount of reinforcement 81
    2. Strength of drive at time of learning 83
    3. Amount of reward 83
    4. Interval between instrumental act and goal response 84
    5. Frequency of reinforcement 84
    6. Punishment 85
    7. Sub-goal reinforcement 86
    8. Hierarchical position of habits 86
    9. Generalization 87
    10. Interval between learning and extinction 87
    11. Effect of previous extinctions 88
    12. Strength of drive at time of extinction 89
  Instrumental act regression 89
    1. Shock frustration 90
    2. Removal of reward 93
    3. Satiation 94
    4. Interpretation 94
  Primitivation 96
  Hypnotic age regression 98
  Schizophrenia 100
  Conclusions 102

VI. REPRESSION 105
    Infantile amnesia 106
    Measurement of repression 110
        1. The nature of the unpleasant 110
        2. Recall of experiences 111
        3. Associative repression (after-expulsion) 113
    Experimental induction of repression 115
    Conclusions 120
VII. PROJECTION AND DREAMS 121
    Motivationally determined perception 121
    Ideas of reference 122
    Attribution of traits 124
    Dreams 126
        1. Influence of external stimuli 127
        2. Events of the previous day 128
        3. Influence of motives 128
    Conclusions 132
VIII. CONCLUSIONS 133
    Infantile sexuality 135
    Oedipus: a lesson in cultural relativity 136
    Development and regression: the role of learning 137
    Mental mechanisms 139
    The directions of progress 140
BIBLIOGRAPHY 144
INDEX 153

Chapter I

Erotogenesis

FUNDAMENTAL to Freud's whole theory of personality dynamics is the concept of *libido* (1905). Briefly, this notion suggests that the source of energy for all positive affectional attachments is sexual (libidinal), and that therefore the impulse to behave sexually is present in the child at as early an age as is the capacity to love.

This impulse is instinctual in origin and its systematic aspects are badly tangled in the complexities of Freudian metapsychology. No consideration can be given to the validity of the concept per se because to do so would require value judgments as to what kind of a psychological system is most desirable. If a consistent theory is laid down along the lines of psychoanalysis, it must include a concept like libido; conversely, if a concept like libido is to be used, then the whole theoretical system must have some such structure as psychoanalysis.

Quite the contrary is true of the factual basis of libido, however. The validity of Freud's assertions about the *facts* of sex behavior can be determined by reference to other and later sources of information.

According to Freud's description of sexuality in the child, the libido is at first localized in other erotogenic zones than the genital. During the first three or four years of life there is a relative latency of genital sexuality and an activation of behavior designed to secure gratification through the oral and anal zones. The connection between these pregenital and the later genital activities is the quality of pleasure and gratification gained from them; Freud's contention is that the sensations arising from stimulation of all three zones are fundamentally the same and that there are similarities too great for coincidence in the kinds of behavior oriented toward them. Examples of this are to be seen in intentional manipulation, orgastic reactions, and reactions to deprivation.

A second significant aspect of infantile sexuality is its autoerotic quality. The sexual impulse is not attached to an object in the outer world; there is no object cathexis, as is normally the case from the fourth or fifth year. The child's own body serves as an object for the reduction of "sensitivity" of the erotogenic zones, and the aim of all self-manipulation, whether pregenital or genital, is to gain the appropriate pleasurable sensations from the zones.

The particular character of the three zones is in part a function of learning, according to Freud, in the sense that the oral zone secures its erotogenic quality as a result of constant stimulation during the pleasurable activity of sucking at the breast or bottle (1905, p. 45). The thumb as an object for gratification of oral craving, by thumbsucking, likewise attains its status as a gratifying object by being used for pleasure. The learning of anal erotism functions similarly (1905, p. 47).

ORAL EROTISM

1. *Thumbsucking.* The chief technique for gaining oral gratification, utilized by the neonate and very young infant (1 to 3 months), is pleasure-sucking at the nipple or at some part of its own body. It is impossible to validate Freud's assumptions about the pleasure-giving quality of the sensations derived from such stimulation, but experimental and observational studies of the sucking reflex and of behavior organized around stimulation of the oral zone support the

general proposition that infants not only seek opportunity for such stimulation independently of the feeding process but also show orgastic and deprivational behavior. The seeking for stimulation when deprived suggests that there is a drive to gain gratification from oral stimulation.

The sucking reflex is present at birth and has even been observed before the child is fully born. As is the case with most native behavior, there is an improvement in its accuracy and efficiency with experience. It can be elicited at birth by touching the cheeks, chin, or lips, according to Pratt, Nelson, and Sun (1930), but the required kind of stimulation becomes more specific within two weeks and the lips themselves must normally be touched thereafter. In general the reflex occurs more readily when the child is hungry and when he is awake.

Springing from this innate activity is a complex set of activities the consequences of which are to provide objects for the repetitive stimulation of the lip area. Blanton (1917) observed occasional fingersucking immediately after birth and Halverson (1938) reports the occurrence of nonrewarded sucking or mouthing at the nipple following eating after the first six weeks, while thumbsucking occurred even earlier. Such pleasure-sucking (nonnutritional) was often at a somewhat more rapid rate than the previous milk-sucking had been, and Halverson suggests that this was due to the fact that the child did not have to take time to swallow. The rate of sucking with difficult, slow-flowing nipples was likewise greater than that with easy nipples, a further confirmation of this interpretation. Swallowing does not commonly occur with air- or thumbsucking.

With increasing age and manipulability of the extremities there is greater frequency of pleasure-sucking and a greater proportion of it utilizes the thumbs or fingers rather than the bottle or breast. Levy (1928) found that the habit started, in the majority of instances, during the first 3 months, and Macfarlane (1939) has given evidence that it decreases again between 21 months and 60 months; in her group of 252 Berkeley children about 28 per cent did some thumbsucking at the earlier age and this was reduced to half by the later. This frequency is comparable to that of Levy, who reported a maximum of 25.4 per cent.

On the whole, evidence supports Freud's view (1905, pp. 44-46) that thumbsucking is a reaction to deprivation. It occurs not uncommonly when the nipple is withdrawn from an infant's mouth and its chief antecedent condition, as a habitual activity, is inadequacy of opportunity to suck extensively in connection with the eating process. The most complete analysis of this aspect of orality is that of Levy (1928). The data of his study were obtained by questioning the mothers of 122 children of various ages. The results are, therefore, open to the customary errors of recall and of unskilled observation that naturally inhere in any information secured from parents about events that were not at the time observed with an intention of recall later. The detailed character of the recollections of duration of eating periods, usual intervals between feedings, and reactions to feeding, as well as the number of frank admissions of inability to recall, led Levy to place considerable confidence in the data, however, and there is little reason for assuming that any serious constant error crept in.

Of the 122 children, 25.4 per cent were reported to have done some finger- or thumbsucking for pleasure. This figure compares reasonably well with the data of various other studies cited by Levy. An additional 16.1 per cent used pacifiers other than their own bodies. These were mainly chewed rather than sucked. Since the data related to an unspecified age designated in a general way as infancy, it is impossible to tell the exact age relations of these two kinds of activity, chewing and sucking, although the majority of cases of thumbsucking were known to have started during the first 3 months. None of the children who used artificial pacifiers were thumbsuckers; the objects of pleasure-seeking appear to

TABLE 1. Frequency of fingersucking among 122 children having various degrees of opportunity for sucking during the regular feeding process. (Summarized from Levy, 1928, p. 910)

Adequacy of opportunity for sucking while feeding	No. of finger-suckers	No. of non-finger-suckers
Satisfactory		
Spontaneous withdrawal by child	8	93
Unsatisfactory		
Spontaneous withdrawal too quickly	6	0
Spontaneous withdrawal, but unsatisfied	5	0
Forced withdrawal; time-limited feeding	7	1
Feeding by dropper	2	0
Total	28	94

have been *fixed* by some process, or it might be said that an object cathexis had been formed.

A comparison of fingersuckers and nonfingersuckers showed a difference in the amount of opportunity for sucking during the feeding process itself (Table 1). The fingersuckers had, on the whole, finished eating much more quickly either because of rigid- and short-timing of the eating period by the mother or because there was customarily a very rapid flow of milk from the breast and the child therefore became quickly satiated with food. There were also, among the fingersuckers, a larger number of youngsters who had had their feeding schedules changed at an early age so that there were fewer feedings and longer intervals between feedings. This does not mean they got less food, because eating-by-sucking increases in speed and efficiency as the child ages. A comparison of the frequency of fingersucking in children on four-hour schedules with that of those on self-schedules showed a slightly but not reliably larger number in the former group.

The nonfingersuckers in these comparisons include the children who used pacifiers. The picture is not a clear cut if these are put in the fingersucker group. Only 4 of the 18 had had the kind of inadequacies in sucking accompanying eating that the majority of fingersuckers had. The main conclusion is still supported, however; fingersuckers, as compared with nonfingersuckers and children who chewed on pacifiers, had histories of greater deprivation of opportunity to suck during the feeding process.

To supplement these findings with better controlled conditions of observation, Levy (1934) compared the frequency of body-sucking and the sucking of a proffered finger by puppies having different amounts of opportunity for sucking. A litter of six animals was taken at birth. One pair, the *long-feeders,* were fed by bottle with a small hole in the nipple and after each meal were allowed to suck to satiety on a nipple covered finger. During the 20 days of the experiment they averaged 62 and 67 minutes of sucking per 24 hours. The *short-feeders* were fed with a large-holed nipple and were not given a finger to suck afterward. They averaged 21 and 22 minutes of sucking per 24 hours. The third pair from the litter, the *breast feeders,* were left with the bitch. The short-feeders gave evidence of sucking deprivation by chewing and sucking at each other's bodies between meals, and by being far more responsive to a proffered finger between meals than were the long-feeders. The latter were responsive to the finger just before meals but not at other times. The breast feeders were never responsive to the finger and did no body sucking. The significance of the latter point is not clear, but the comparison of the long- and short-feeders seems to support Levy's findings on the previous study—namely, that sucking independent of the eating process is at least in part a function of deprivation of opportunity to suck in connection with eating.

Freud (1905, p. 45) suggested that the lips became the locus of sensations that required sucking to dissipate them because sucking accompanied the highly pleasurable taking of nourishment. This proposition might be converted into this statement: pleasure-sucking is a function of practice at sucking in association with eating. No direct evidence is available with reference to this point, but Pratt, Nelson, and Sun (1930) found that the sucking reaction to liquid on the tongue decreased in frequency during the first two weeks of life if the liquid was administered by a medicine dropper that did not touch the mouth. On the contrary, there was some slight (but inconclusive) evidence of an increase in sucking when the drops were presented with an applicator that always touched the lips. This evidence is of little importance, however, in view of the same authors' findings that there is an increasing restriction, with age, of the areas in which stimulation can produce the sucking reflex. If the practice factor is important in developing pleasure-sucking, it must be very influential on the first few trials, since all observers agree that such behavior is to be found during the first weeks of life.

Whether the term *masturbatory* is to be applied to finger-sucking (Freud, 1905, p. 46) is a matter more of linguistics than of psychology. It is clear that infants as well as older children seek opportunity for stimulating the lips and eliciting the sucking reflex. When the finger rather than the mother's breast is used as the stimulating object, the process may reasonably be called self-stimulation, i.e., masturbation. The same may be said for air-sucking from an empty bottle.

The effects on behavior of interrupting fingersucking are

various. They include quiet acceptance, weak or strong efforts at resumption, crying, and efforts to turn the head toward other objects. These are the conventional signs of frustration of drive-instigated behavior. Unfortunately we do not have a complete description of such activity for comparison with Halverson's (1938) description of behavior following interference with nutritional sucking during bottle feeding. What clinical observations there are, however, permit no doubt that fingersucking is often strongly motivated.

That it is relatively independent of the stimulus of hunger is indicated by the findings of Jensen (1932), who reports that 10 of his infants sucked on air continuously for 15 minutes after finishing a feeding and then were quiet until the next regular feeding. He secured 30 observations of this behavior. This, taken in conjunction with Halverson's observations and Levy's study of the short-feeder puppies, points rather definitely to Freud's contention that the pleasure-sucking is detached early in the infant's life and henceforth can provide gratification independent of that provided by nutritional sucking or the ingestion of food.

In summary, it may be said that the rather meager data cited here *support* Freud's views in the following respects:

1. Nonnutritional sucking, either of the food source or of the fingers, seems to be motivated by some drive other than hunger.

2. The degree of independence of nonnutritional sucking from the hunger drive is unknown, but since such sucking occurs with greater frequency when a child is hungry, the degree of independence cannot be total.

3. The effects of deprivation are similar to such effects with other drives.

The data are *insufficient* to throw light on the following points:

1. Nonnutritional sucking develops as a consummatory response by virtue of the association between sucking and eating.

2. Nonnutritional sucking has a strong orgastic effect. (Jensen's data are suggestive, but no more; studies of the substitutive value of nonnutritional sucking are badly needed.)

3. Fingersucking is a preferred form of nonnutritional sucking because of its autoerotic quality; i.e., the fingers have taken on erotic properties as a consequence of chance encounters and the child therefore gains double pleasure, part from fingers and part from mouth. Levy's finding that children who used their fingers did not use pacifiers is suggestive but scarcely conclusive because of the nature of the methods by which his data were obtained.

The two latter problems could be solved without great difficulty by appropriate observations. The first one would require somewhat elaborate modification of the early eating habits and might better be studied in puppies. In any case, it seems clear that a great deal of light could be thrown on the development of this component of the libido by relatively slight effort.

2. *Nailbiting.* Although Freud did not include nailbiting in his discussion of infantile oral stimulation, the compulsive character of the behavior has suggested to Wechsler (1931) that it may be a masturbatory equivalent deriving from an incomplete adjustment to the shift from pregenital to genital sexuality. Like thumbsucking, it is peculiarly difficult to eliminate and for this reason may be supposed to have some rather unusual and fundamental motivation.

The incidence of nailbiting is a function of age. In a group of 252 children, Macfarlane (1939) found evidence of it in not more than 10 per cent during the first 42 months. There was a sharp increase during the following 6 months to about 25 per cent. By 60 months there was a decrease to 17 per cent. The relationship here to frequency of thumbsucking appears to be a negative one. The method of observation is not described, but since these children were being studied as part of a larger program, both direct observation and parental report were undoubtedly used. Wechsler (1931) examined the fingernails of 3025 New York City public nursery and school children and found no instances in a group of 31 children under 3 years. After 3 years, however, there was a rapid increase to about 30 per cent (boys = 29.4; girls = 30.9) at 6 years. The next important increase occurred between 11 and 12 for the girls (43.7 per cent) and between 13 and 14 for the boys (43.6 per cent). By 17 years the girls had reduced to 15.9 per cent but the boys to 27.9 per cent only. These figures are similar, for both the elementary and early high school years, to those obtained by Billig (1941), except that Billig did not find the sharp decrease in girls at the tenth-grade level (ages 16-17 in Wechsler's study).

Olson (1936) has criticized Wechsler's technique of observation on the grounds that as girls get older they begin to manicure their nails. Further, he has demonstrated that while the reliability of judgment by two observers, with reference to the presence or absence of nailbiting, is fairly satisfactory (+.82), the validity of the method is open to criticism. He compared the frequency of observed nailbiting during 20 5-minute observation periods in children who were judged to show and not to show signs on their fingernails. The 2 groups had almost identical average frequency of both biting and oral movements in general. It must be recognized, therefore, that presence of nail disfigurement cannot be used as a measure of frequency of oral stimulation; at best it can represent, and only roughly, the presence or absence of one form of oral stimulation.

The original causes of nailbiting are unknown. Billig (1941) questioned 89 nailbiters from the fourth, fifth, and sixth grades about the origin of the practice. The majority reported that they had learned it from someone else, a mother, sibling, or friend, and then presumably had been unable to stop.

The immediate stimulus to biting was reported to be fear, excitement, nervousness and self-consciousness; motion pictures, exciting games and difficult tests were prominent among the sources of the excitement or nervousness. Any interpretation of these stimuli in sexual terms would be purely gratuitous.

Billig reports that no more than 75 per cent of a group of elementary school nailbiters could be cured by application of quassia solution, but he considers this proportion to have been a function of the children's desire, or lack of it, to stop.

These various findings are suggestive of a behavior mechanism somewhat similar to that of thumbsucking. The resistance to modification indicates a strongly motivated response having an oral orientation. The attitude of seriousness and concentration during the act, and the reaction of guilt at being caught, that Billig describes, are strongly reminiscent of thumbsucking, too. Beyond this implication of gratification of a strong motive, the data do not support or invalidate psychoanalytic theory.

3. *Oral gestures.* In addition to thumbsucking and nailbiting there are many other gestures and nervous movements that involve either touching or manipulating some part of the mouth. The study of such behavior was initiated by Olson (1929) with his use of the method of short sample observation. This method gives a measurement of the frequency of a given form of action in terms of the proportion of observation periods in which it occurs. Thus if an observer counted

the presence or absence of thumbsucking during 10 5-minute periods and found it to occur 1 or more times in 6 of those periods, the score for that child would be 60 per cent. This frequency may be interpreted either as a measure of *strength* of the habit, as Olson has done, or as an indication of the amount of either stimulation or activity that occurs. The interpretation will naturally depend on the theoretical use to which the data are to be put.

The incidence of oral gestures, including thumbsucking and nailbiting, in comparison with those centering around other parts of the body, is relatively high in children from 3 years up. Measurements are not available for the earlier years. From 6 to 14 years, Olson's data (1929, pp. 38-39) show that there is no consistent change in frequency, and data for college students gave approximately the same frequency.

By comparing the frequency on two different occasions, Olson was able to get a measure of the constancy of the activity. He found that there was virtually no change after 8 days, but that as progressively longer periods were allowed to intervene between the 2 measures, there was less and less constancy. Coefficients of correlation corrected for attenuation varied from .98 for 8 days to .46 for 1 year. Children evidently do show a certain individual consistency for considerable periods of time.

The genesis of such behavior was sought by Olson in imitation of siblings or schoolroom neighbors, breast feeding, fatigue and nutritional status. The influence of siblings was measured by a correlational technique. Like-sex siblings proved to be slightly more similar in frequency than unlike-sex ones; the same was true for like- and unlike-sex twins, although there were only 6 cases of each kind. By correlating the frequency of each child with the average of the five children seated in best view of him in the schoolroom, it was found that only slight evidence of a relationship existed. This figure varied from +.45 to −.57 for the 15 schoolrooms measured; the median coefficient is but .07. The *size* of the coefficients in the different rooms correlated −.78, however, with the number of seating changes that had occurred in each room during the preceding three months, i.e., the correlations were highest in those rooms in which the environment of each child had been most stable.

The data concerning breast feeding permit the correlation, for 29 cases, of the frequency of oral gestures at preschool age with duration of breast feeding. Since there was no information on the amount of bottle feeding, the findings are of no significance.

Olson also compared the frequency of all kinds of gestures, oral included, in the morning and in the afternoon in order to determine the effect of fatigue. The results were ambiguous, with a slight but scarcely reliable tendency for greater movement in the afternoon.

In order to get a measure of nutritional status, the ponderal index was used; this is weight divided by height. The larger the index, the fatter is the person. Correlation of this index with frequency of oral gestures, as well as comparison of normal school children with a group that had been allocated to an open air school because of poor weight, indicated not a large but, at all ages from 7 to 13 years and for both sexes, a negative relation between goodness of nutritional status and frequency of oral movements. In other words, the children who were undernourished, for whatever reason, had most oral movements. Among the older children (ages 10-12), however, there was a curvilinear relation of some magnitude; the overweight children also were high in movements. For this reason it may be suggested that those children who deviate decidedly from the norm, and hence find their physical and social adjustment a little more difficult, have more worry and fear; therefore, as was the case with nailbiting, they show more oral signs of agitation. On the other hand, the possibility cannot be ignored that the same factors that lead to undernourishment (either poor eating or poor assimilation) may be responsible for the greater amount of stimulation and manipulation of the oral area.

Other factors than the nutritional can influence the frequency of oral gestures, however. Jones (1942) observed 25 high school boys while they were doing mental arithmetic. He used a short time-sample technique similar to Olson's. A comparison of frequencies with those obtained during appropriate control periods showed that oral gestures were sharply increased in all subjects by this task. Various other categories also showed increases, the manual and head being among the larger along with the oral. These results suggest that oral movements are by no means uniquely symptomatic of inherent oral erotism.

These various studies indicate the importance of nonoral stimulation in determining the frequency of oral gestures. Further, the factors of imitation and learning from others must be taken into account in explaining their origin. Obviously there can be little learning of behavior that carries no reward value whatever, and this finding, therefore, does not carry with it any negation of the general principle derived from the study of thumbsucking and nailbiting that these acts have drive-instigation. So far is Freud supported. Beyond this, the data serve no more the purposes of the present analysis than to indicate that the Freudian theory is oversimplified.

ANAL EROTISM

The basic observation that appears to have led Freud (1905, pp. 46-47) to postulate an erotic property to anal sensations was his clinically noted correlation between constipation or other bowel disorders in childhood and adult nervousness. Koch (1935) has obtained data which give some slight though indirect support for this observation. She observed 46 nursery children during a school year and obtained a highly reliable measure of the frequency of nervous gestures in each child. A measure of constipation was secured by parental ratings. The correlations of the latter with oral movements and with total number of movements in boys, but not in girls, were sufficiently large (.39 and .61 respectively) to suggest a relationship beyond chance. Whether frequency of mannerisms is in any sense a measure of what Freud meant by "nervousness," even in adults, is an open question. An alternative interpretation, the one given by Koch, is that fear and anger reduce gastrointestinal motility and also cause the emotional tension that eventuates in nervous gestures or mannerisms.

GENITAL EROTISM

Freud's emphasis on the autoerotic character of early sex behavior is especially relevant to genital activity, since of the three erotic sources it is the one that most commonly takes on a social orientation in the adult. Unlike oral habits such as thumbsucking, however, genital masturbation increases rather than decreases with age and therefore there is an increase in both autoerotic and object-directed genital sexuality.

That the genital organs are susceptible to stimulation in early infancy is beyond question. In the male, the erectile tissue of the penis is responsive, and "spontaneous" erections have been observed by Blanton (1917) at birth.

The most elaborate observations of the phenomena of penial tumescence and detumescence have been made by Halverson (1940). Nine male infants varying in age from 3 to 20 weeks were observed for 8.5 consecutive hours per day for 10 days. They were placed on their backs in their cribs, naked, and the cribs were ranged in a semicircle in front of the observer, who recorded all his observations on a time-sample blank. The conditions of observation and recording were such that considerable reliance may be placed on the findings.

Tumescence occurred at least once on every day with 7 of the children and on 9 and 8 days respectively for the other 2. There were great individual differences in frequency, however, the actual number of T's (tumescence) varying from a median of 4 to a median of 35 per day. Many of these were closely linked in time and several T's often seemed to form a series. Among the 9 boys, the median number of series per day varied from 3 to 11. The average duration of series of T's varied from 2.4 to 14.5 minutes. The maximum duration for any single T was 66 minutes. The time intervals between series of T's varied from 10 to 320 minutes. T occurred during sleep as well as waking and frequently awakened the infant.

The effects of these tumescence reactions on the children were fairly marked, for the most part, and seemed to be decidedly disturbing. The 636 series of T were accompanied by various manifestations: restlessness, fretting or crying on 371 occasions, and stretching or flexing the legs stiffly on 169 occasions. The rest of the instances were accompanied by slight stirring or else the child was quiet—91 times. On 5 occasions thumbsucking occurred.

These kinds of actions indicate only inferentially that tumescence was *unpleasant,* of course, but the contrast with detumescence is striking. The latter was accompanied by crying on only 33 occasions and frequently occurred during sleep. In more than two thirds of the instances of this latter, the child did not awake. In general, the behavior following detumescence seemed to represent playful activity or relaxation.

That this behavior denotes a feeling of *pleasure* is, again, purely inferential, but nothing more than inference can ever be used for verification of the relationship between feeling and behavior in young infants who have no language with which to report on the former.

It should not prove surprising that children would themselves learn to perform an act that reduced the restlessness and crying. By trial and error, through random movements of one sort or another, the child may learn to manipulate the area that he discovers is the source of the disturbing stimulation. Since coordination is poor at first, direct manual masturbation in the form of holding, pressing, or stroking is not often observed during the first months, although Halverson did observe a few instances of grasping at the penis, but Levy (1928) found on questioning the mothers of 49 male children that such activity had been noted in 26 cases during the first three years; 19 of the 26 were observed during the first 18 months. In a group of 26 girls only 4 cases of genital touching were reported, but Levy points out that nonmanual manipulation by thigh-rubbing or squeezing is difficult to detect in girls. Since these data are reports by parents who had made no systematic observations and who must have had varying amounts of resistance to either recall of the instances or report about them, some scepticism about the accuracy of the figures must be expressed. It is probably safe to conclude no more than that masturbation is common among male infants and not so common among female.

This sex difference is supported by Koch (1935), who found a reliably greater frequency of masturbatory activities in preschool boys than girls during 400 half-minute observation periods spread two per day over 8 months. The frequency for both was extremely low, however; the mean for the 21 boys was 2.31 with a S. D. of the distribution of 3.35, and for the 25 girls it was .78 with a S. D. of .45. The critical ratio is 2.07. Dr. Koch points out that there was an even greater difference between the sexes in frequency of hair manipulation, the girls being higher in this case. The critical ratio was 5.64. This suggests that the anatomical nature of the stimulated area may be of crucial significance in determining these kinds of self-manipulatory behavior; the girls' longer hair and the boys' more prominently structured genitalia may well provide for important sex differences of a more general sort than those deriving from the single sexual anatomical distinction. A comparison of the relative frequency of breast-oriented movements in postpubescent boys and girls would be interesting in this connection. However, before Koch's findings can be given clear interpretation, some control of tightness of clothing must be secured; the irritant qualities of tight pants on growing boys may be of major importance here as a stimulant to penial tumescence.

These various data are supportive of Freud's clinical observations on three scores: first, the existence of extensive genital sensitivity, stimulation and activity from birth; second, the frequency of infantile masturbation in the male; and third, the relative infrequency of manual masturbation in the female. There is no evidence relevant to his assertion that self-stimulation is universal for both sexes and that the female develops nonmanual techniques. Completely lacking, too, is information on the alleged diminution of early infantile masturbation and a resurgence later at ages 4 to 6.

THE EROTOGENIC COMPLEX

The partial impulses arising from the various erotogenic zones are relatively independent of one another at first, according to Freud (1905, pp. 56-57), but in the course of development become unified into the genital sexual impulse. Freud is insistent, however, that all partial impulses are essentially sexual from the very beginning. The exact interrelations of the components of this erotogenic complex have never been made entirely clear, but they are apparently different aspects of a single impulse. For example, when regression from adult heterosexuality occurs, it is sometimes a kind of pleasure-seeking that is characteristic of one of these infantile components (Freud, 1920). But the quantitative relations between them are uncertain; it is impossible to say, for instance, whether positive or negative correlations between strength of oral and anal impulses would support the theory. The one thing clear is that there is hypothesized to be a complex of interrelated erotogenic zones and that this interrelationship is a function of activity instigated by them. So much, too, is supported by observational data.

1. *Oral components.* Within the oral impulse two aspects may be distinguished (Freud, 1933, pp. 136-137): the sucking or incorporative and the biting or sadistic. These occur chronologically in this order. Data to support this observation come from two studies, those of Levy (1928) and of Macfarlane (1939). Levy found that 18 of the 122 children in his investigation used pacifiers of some sort and that they customarily bit or chewed on them. None of these children was a thumbsucker, according to the mothers' reports. Macfarlane found that as reports of thumbsucking decreased in a group of 252 children from 21 to 60 months, reports of nailbiting increased, the sharpest rise coming at 48 months. There appeared to be a negative correlation between the two activities so far as the *group* was concerned, but there is no information on the relation within individual children. In any case, the data from both studies are of insufficient accuracy to

have value in connection with the present problem. The problem of *teething* has not been adequately considered in either the theoretical or empirical analyses.

2. *Simultaneous stimulation*. Whether, as Freud suggests, the unity of partial sexual impulses is innate or is a function of experience is impossible to tell. As will be shown, the conditions for such a unification, through simultaneous stimulation and response, are present from birth.

In the series of observations of male infants described above in connection with genital erotism, Halverson (1940) recorded micturition, defecation, thumbsucking, sleeping, etc., as well as the occurrence of tumescence (T) and detumescence (D). These activities are by no means all incompatible with one another and on many occasions two or more occurred in conjunction.

The frequency of association of tumescence with micturition or defecation was high; T accompanied 61 per cent of the observed instances of the former and 49 per cent of the latter. As was the case with both eliminative actions, T was most common during the three hours after eating. In most instances the T developed shortly before the eliminative act. So far as sucking was concerned, Halverson (1938) found that contented feeding was never accompanied by T; by "contented" was meant easy sucking, neither too fast nor too slow, unhampered by any restrictive conditions. Hampered feeding, induced by a small-holed nipple, or by lack of milk, was not infrequently accompanied by T. On these occasions considerable straining of the abdominal muscles was noticeable, and Halverson concluded that all tumescence was a consequence of abdominal pressure on the bladder. In the case of hampered sucking this was produced by straining, and in the eliminative actions by fullness of the viscera.

From a theoretical standpoint the detumescence is of even

greater interest. *D* normally occurred shortly after elimination had taken place or after sucking had either stopped or returned to normal. Since *T* created difficulty in the eliminative function, and hence discomfort, the elimination had frequently to be painful. With *D* occurring afterward, however, there was presumably a reduction in discomfort and certainly a relaxation and quiescence. If this represented a species of gratification similar to that reported by adults, this state of affairs was preceded by excitation from the anal or urethral areas or from the frustrated sucking activity. These three sources of stimulation, then, are clearly shown to be presented in such fashion, in earliest infancy, as to permit their becoming the conditioned stimuli to relaxation and quiescence. This is essentially the kind of behavior that first led Freud to posit a unity to the various partial impulses.

In conclusion it may be said that although there are various alternative physiological hypotheses to account for the correlation of penial tumescence and detumescence with the onset and decline of stimulation arising from the anal, urethral and frustrated oral activities, the behavior facts are clear that 1) genital excitation occurs frequently and from birth, and 2) it accompanies excitation from the anatomical areas of the other partial impulses. Data are lacking on the "orgasm quality" of detumescence, but 3) reduction of tumescence produces a definite relaxation immediately following both elimination and the cessation of frustrated sucking.

CONCLUSIONS

The notion of erotogenesis boils down to little more than the presumption that several sources of pleasurable stimulation are somehow related to one another. In working out the details of this relation, Freud first applied the properties of adult genital sexuality to infantile activities centered around the oral and anal-urethral body zones and then assumed that there was a specific quantum of pleasure-seeking that could be channelized through the various zones, making one a substitute for another. The evidence cited here supports the general correctness of the first point, but throws less light on the latter.

Self-stimulation of the oral zone appears to be a form of drive-instigated behavior that is not entirely independent of the eating process. It does represent consummatory activity in its own right, however, and interference with such forms as thumbsucking and nailbiting produces typical frustration reactions. The source of this drive, if it can be so called, is not clear; its early appearance suggests a native origin but there is no proof that amount of practice does not influence its strength.

The functional relationship of substitutability between the various zones has not been demonstrated, but the observational data on infant boys show that the conditions may be present for such a unity to develop. In any case, genital and pregenital behavior occur with sufficient profusion to support (but not critically) almost any hypothesis involving a positive relationship between them.

Chapter II

Erotic Behavior of Children

PREGENITAL SEXUALITY

BEHAVIOR having a social orientation, or at least a quality of being exhibited persistently to other people, is organized around the oral and eliminative functions very early in life. Playful manipulation of the lips, biting and spitting, and a definitely vocal interest in toilet activities occur in the majority of children at one time or another during the first three years. These actions are important indicators of pregenital erotism and define that motivational source as having definite social relevance.

Unhappily, there is little to be learned, by the direct observation of children, about the relation of pregenital to genital erotism or behavior. The most extensive study is that of Susan Isaacs (1933), who noted in detail all pregenital, genital, aggressive and competitive behavior exhibited by 31 English children in a nursery school. The observations covered a period of approximately 3 years, from 1924 to 1927. The children were in the school for varying lengths of time, and their ages ranged from 2-3 to 6-5 (except for an 8-year-old boy and a 10-year-old girl) at the beginning of the observations. Their "mean mental ratio" was 131. Of the group, 25 were boys. The majority of these children were from professional homes at Cambridge and although some were considered to be "difficult" (problem) children, others of the group were fairly typical of their part of society.

The nature of the data prevented a statistical statement of frequency of different kinds of behavior, and the anecdotal method of presentation precludes even a rough estimate of the age ranges within which each kind of behavior fell most characteristically. Indeed, the chief result of the investigation appears to have been the recording of such a tremendous number of instances of behavior organized around oral, anal, urethral, and genital functions and ideas that Freud may be freed forevermore of any charge of overestimating the frequency of such behavior.

A few examples of the kinds of incidents noted will suggest the richness of Mrs. Isaacs' data.

Oral:

George and Frank, having climbed up to the window overlooking the lane, to see a motor, began to spit on to the window; Dan joined in; they all spat vigorously, and said, "Look at it running down." George also spoke of "belly," and Frank of "ah-ah lu-lu," and "bim-bom," both laughing. (p. 113)

When Priscilla, Frank and Duncan were playing with the puppy, Priscilla said something about "sucking that," obviously referring to the dog's penis. Duncan said, "Oh, you dirty thing." Frank laughed. Priscilla said, "and get milk." Duncan: "You don't get milk from dogs!" Someone asked where one did get milk. Duncan replied, "From cows and goats." (p. 114)

Anal and urethral:

Dan's mother reported that this afternoon, when she was carrying him on the return from a walk, he had asked her, "Shall I make water on you?" She said, "Do you want to make water? I'll put you down." "No, on *you,* shall I?" (p. 121)

The children were getting water to drink in cups, and Harold told the others that he had given Frank some "wee-wee water" to drink. He often says "there's wee-wee water in the bowl" in which he washes his hands. Later he said he had drunk "wee-wee water," and that the water in the cups was that.

Frank said, "Shall we make Benjie drink wee-wee water?"

"Yes," Harold said, "and poison him." And another time, "and make spots come out all over him." (p. 122)

Frank and some others were looking at a picture, and Frank suddenly hit it, and said, "I smacked its bottie."

Harold told Mrs. I. that George "wee-wee'd" in the garden "always." (p. 123)

While resting, Frank and George had taken their socks off. Frank said to George, "I can see your big toe," with a giggle; whereupon George immediately pulled his penis out. (p. 135)

Sexual curiosity:

When the children were playing a family game with the puppy as baby, Duncan said: "Undress him." Priscilla: "Yes." Duncan: "and then we can see his bim-bom;" there was great laughter and excitement among the children and all repeated, "see his bim-bom." Priscilla undid the rug in which he was wrapped and called others to look: "Come on, come on, look underneath." The puppy stood on its hind legs near Priscilla. Duncan: "Oh, he tried to get to your what-d'ye-call-it." (p. 141)

Jane and Conrad went with Mrs. I. to the ethnological museum today. When looking at a human figure made of bamboo, Conrad pointed out the prominent penis, giggling, and saying, "What is that funny thing, sticking out? We know, don't we?" They whispered and giggled about it. (p. 142)

The significance of these observations lies in four things:

1. They support Freud's contention (1905, p. 34) that such activities are very common among normal children of preschool age.

2. The ages at which different kinds of activity are noted indicate that the children may be called polymorphous perverse, but in the social milieu there is no rigid sequence of development (sucking to biting, expelling to retaining, etc.) of the different partial impulses. (Cf. Freud, 1933, pp. 134-140.)

3. Behavior having exhibitionism and voyeurism as its aim is common at 3 and 4 years of age (Freud, 1905, p. 52), but while sadistic (cruel, aggressive) behavior is also common, masochistic behavior is relatively infrequent.

4. The "shame and loathing" of which Freud speaks (1905, p. 21, p. 51) as the motives toward relinquishing infantile sexual aims are evident in connection with both pregenital and genital behavior; i.e., the children showed similar giggling, embarrassed shouting, and defiant aggressiveness for displays of both kinds of interests or actions. So far as the interrelationship between genital and pregenital is concerned,

there seems to be no other evidence in the social behavior beyond this fact that both kinds are reacted to as if they were forbidden. Freud (1920, ch. 20) commented on the anonymous obstetrician who found nothing "sexual" about childbirth because there was nothing nasty about it. The present data make it appear that a large number of activities (oral, anal, urethral, genital, voyeuristic, sadistic, exhibitionistic, etc.) give a similar appearance of being "bad" (forbidden), and Freud's sarcasm to the contrary notwithstanding, *the behavior itself does not indicate any other relationship between them.*

The observation of children in a nursery school is not entirely satisfactory for the study of these various kinds of forbidden behavior, however; the youngsters are under supervision for but a few hours during the day and no matter how lenient the teachers may be, there is still some restriction on behavior. For these reasons the recall of *childhood experiences by adults* suggests itself as a supplementary technique. This is the psychoanalytic method, in essence.

The difficulties encountered with recall are different from those of direct observation, but they are no less serious. The events of childhood are poorly remembered (for many reasons, not for just one) and there is great danger that in the search for forgotten items, the examiner or analyst may suggest the memories that are to be recalled, or more recent phantasies or experiences may be falsely allocated as to time. On the other hand, if an adult is not put under pressure of strong motivation, his recall may be incomplete. The data of psychoanalysis, therefore, require some validation from different techniques of recall that eliminate certain of these errors.

The most detailed recall of childhood experiences, obtained under relatively objective conditions, was that of G. V.

Hamilton (1929) in connection with his study of marriage. Two hundred adults, a hundred of each sex, all of whom were or had been married, answered nearly 400 questions that had been typed on separate cards. The purpose of this method of presentation was to avoid either suggestion or undue pressure from the examiner as well as indications of satisfaction or dissatisfaction from him. Hamilton was seeking to keep the recall as independent of the examiner as possible.

Among the questions asked (pp. 447-448) were the following: 1) It is probable that children normally pass through a period during which they find sensual delight in various kinds of nasty thoughts, words, and acts. Give an account of any of your nastinesses of childhood. 2) Do you recall whether or not, as a child, you were fond of prolonging the act of moving your bowels for the sake of pleasant thrills which this gave you? 3) Did voiding urine give you the same kind of pleasure? In answer to the first, about a fifth of the men and a sixth of the women were able to recall scatological interests. To the other two questions approximately two thirds of the men and three fourths of the women gave negative replies.

Since memory for all childhood events is relatively poor and no special aids to recall were used these data are not easy of interpretation. The questions are themselves positively suggestive, however, and should tend to increase positive answers. Whatever the accuracy of recall may have been, it is evident that a good number of people had actively sought gratification through pregenital channels.

A number of questions (pp. 449-466) designed to elicit recall of exhibitionistic, voyeuristic, sadistic, masochistic, and narcissistic experiences or interests were presented and the answers to each indicated that these kinds of behavior, too, were far from rare in the remembered childhood.

Such recollections, along with the direct observations of children's behavior, give strong support to what were, in reality, *clinical observations* by Freud. Children clearly seek organic satisfactions, their interests are coordinated with such motivation, and they show the anxieties and surreptitiousness that would be expected in a society that does not condone such activity.

GENITAL SEXUALITY

1. *Sex play*. The observations of Isaacs were not limited to pregenital pleasure-seeking behavior. She records a rich sampling of activities organized around genitality and the heterosexual implications of procreation and family life. Persistent curiosity about the anatomy of opposite-sexed persons was expressed by the children, and the boys made repeated approaches toward women in both playful and serious efforts to examine the genitalia. The significance of these observations scarcely goes beyond illustration, however, since neither the antecedents of such behavior nor its relation to other kinds of gratification are in any way indicated.

Hamilton (1929, pp. 330-334) reports that 20 per cent of the 100 women and 13 per cent of the 100 men in his study were able to recall prepubertal sex play with persons of the opposite sex. About half these cases appear to have been voluntary and half the result of aggressions. For maintenance of anonymity of the subject, however, Hamilton has been forced to present the data in such form that actual frequencies are difficult to determine. Such figures are probably of little significance, in any case. Of primary importance is the indication that matters of sex played a part in the childhood activities of at least some of these adults.

Such data as these seem of little relevance to Freudian or any other theory. The fact that so few adults can recall experiences is probably more significant as an indicator of the kind of culture in which they live than of their motivational capacities. Malinowski's observations (1927) show clearly enough that children of preschool age can, under appropriate cultural aegis, be highly active at a genital sexual level and that a large proportion of their social play can be so oriented. But the restrictions of the Trobriand Islander are vastly different from those of recent European and American society, and the freedom from shame and punishment in the former suggests the role that a particular culture has played in determining the Freudian theory of sex development.

2. *Sex curiosity*. Freud's observations (1905, pp. 54-56) concerning the amount and kind of sexual inquisitiveness of small children can be supplemented considerably from recently obtained data of greater breadth. Hattendorf (1932) secured information from mothers about the sex questions their children had asked. A corps of social workers and other trained investigators called on mothers in Minneapolis homes and obtained the data by direct questioning. Many mothers were unable to recall any questions at all but about 1800 children had raised the issue and the relative frequency of different kinds of questions can be determined. Table 2 shows the rank order of these frequencies.

These data confirm Freud's observation that the most frequent question of young children concerns "the riddle of the Sphinx;" between the ages of 2 and 5 years, the commonest questions had to do with the origin of babies. Next in importance are the physical sex differences, and in this connection the absurdity of one of Freud's overgeneralizations becomes evident. According to Freud (1905, p. 54) "It is quite natural for the male child to presuppose in all persons he knows a genital like his own, and to find it impossible to harmonize the lack of it with his conception of others. This conviction is energetically adhered to by the boy and

TABLE 2. Rank order of frequencies with which different types of sex questions were asked by the 1797 children of 981 Minneapolis mothers. N = total number of questions reported. (From Hattendorf, 1932, p. 45)

Types of questions	Ranks at 3 age levels		
	2–5 (N = 865)	6–9 (N = 707)	10–13 (N = 191)
Origin of babies	1	1	2
Coming of another baby	4	2	1
Intra-uterine growth	7	7	8
Birth process	5	3	5
Organs and functions	3	4	3
Physical sex differences	2	4	6
Relation of father to reproduction	6	6	4
Marriage	8	8	7

stubbornly defended against the contradictions which soon result, and is only given up after severe internal struggles (castration complex)." The list of questions given by Hattendorf (1932, pp. 56-57) shows that, on the contrary, there was a very widespread recognition by children of both sexes that there was a physical difference in the genitalia. Only 3 of the 137 questions asked by children 2 to 5 years of age suggested that boys thought the girl's lack of a penis was the result of injury. There is no evidence, either, that girls envied the penis or wished to be boys. The data obviously do not disprove the possibility of such reactions as Freud has described but their universality is not only not demonstrable, but is flatly disproven.

A study of children's attitudes toward sex by Conn (1940) presents somewhat more detailed data concerning the specific reactions of those children who did react with distress to the physical sex difference. Conn used a play technique with 200 children ranging in age from 4 to 12 years; there were 128 boys and 72 girls. About three fourths of the children had seen the genitalia of the opposite sex and about a third of these (*circa* 50) were willing to discuss their reactions via the dolls. The majority indicated a lack of emotional reaction but 17 of the 50 were shocked by it and worried over the cause. Levy (1940) has criticized Conn's conclusion that shock is not universal on the ground that inadequate recall for the older children was not taken into account. Again it must be pointed out that for such a behavior to be universal would require a universal culture pattern. Levy's argument does not seem well taken.

A number of questions indicated confusion as to the way in which babies are born. Indeed, the children's curiosity, even as expressed secondhand through their mothers' verbalizations, indicates a lamentable ignorance of the fundamental biological aspects of procreation.

Although Hattendorf's data do not indicate the anxiety and aversion connected with the process of gaining sexual information, studies by Terman (1938) and Landis *et al.* (1940) do. Terman presented a questionnaire to 792 married couples who were a fairly representative cross section of the California population. The answers were given with strict anonymity and probably are as free from intentional bias as is possible by such a method. Errors of selective recall or repression still remain, of course, but the data give a clear picture nonetheless of repeated frustration of attempts to gain sex information. Of the men, 40 per cent did not disclose their curiosity to adults and another 20 per cent were met with lies and evasions; corresponding figures for the women were 30 per cent and 20 per cent. These figures, coupled with the fact that only 7 per cent of the men and 6 per cent of the women could recall having known the origin of babies before age 6, suggest that the process of gaining information was not easy but that the majority of children had sufficient curiosity to seek some. Landis *et al.* interviewed 143 normal women under unusually favorable conditions, the subjects being aware of the scientific purpose of the interview, and discovered that only 28 per cent considered their childhood sex information adequate. How sex information would compare in these respects with similar curiosity about cows, airplanes, wars, etc., is unknown.

These various data concerning children's sexual curiosity give a picture, in mass, not unlike that briefly described by Freud. They differ, however, in that they are couched in terms of percentages; they relate to measured populations. Freud's clinical observations are in many instances entirely sound, but his findings are purveyed as universals. So much of the nature of sex development is a function of the kinds of rewards and punishments given, of tutelage and stricture, that *no* such generalizations as Freud gives can be considered correct. The ways of behaving inevitably show variation within any one culture, and differences between cultures (cf. Malinowski, 1927; Mead, 1935) are even more sharply defined. The main implications of Freud's description are right; but the quantitative details are wrong and it is from them that implications for the individual case are derived.

3. *Overstimulation and sexual aggressions.* In connection with his discussion of the polymorphous-perverse character of infantile sexuality (1905, p. 51) and the process of fixation (1905, pp. 94-98), Freud says that early or premature genital sex experience conduces to perversion and neurosis. His argument is that the child's sexual instinct is excited to action before the necessary "shame and loathing" for its control are present. Hence, the repression process is weak and the child is unable to resist further sexual gratification. The correlation between perversion, hypersexuality and neurosis on

thé one hand and early sex aggressions or seductions on the other is straightforward from a theoretical standpoint. The same argument might be applied to the other components of the libido; overstimulation of the oral zone in infancy would conduce to later oral activity.

The validity of these observations and conclusions can be tested by reference to the various studies of marriage and of female sexuality in which data concerning early sex experience have been secured.

Unfortunately there are no direct measures of the frequency of perversions in these studies, but Hamilton (1929, p. 342) and Terman (1938, p. 393) have compared the adequacy of orgasm in women with and without the history of occurrence of sex aggressions; a lack of orgasm is considered to be a measure of sexual distortion through inhibition (cf. Chapter 4). Hamilton found that only 35 per cent of his women subjects who had been victims of sex aggressions were able to have adequate orgasms, whereas 70 per cent of those who had no such history were adequate. The difference is 3.7 times its standard error.

Terman's results are in direct contradiction of these findings, however. Of the approximately 250 inadequates, 15 per cent reported sex shock before age 10, while of the 500 adequates, 17 per cent reported such shock, but the difference is entirely unreliable. Shocks occurring after 10 years of age were reported by 19 per cent of the inadequates and by only 14 per cent of the adequates. This difference is in the opposite direction but it, too, is unreliable.

Landis et al. (1940, p. 310) were able to make a more elaborate comparison. They divided their normal and abnormal women subjects into two groups, those who had a history of definite sex aggressions and those who had no experiences or else only explorations and sex play that they had themselves initiated or permitted. The abnormal group included de-mentia precox and manic depressive psychotics as well as psychopathic personalities and neurotics; it is not possible, therefore, to test specifically Freud's notion that sex aggres-sion creates neurosis. There is no reliable difference, however, between the normals and abnormals in the frequency of *re-port* of such experiences.

The history-of-aggression group did have a reliably larger number of women who reported an attitude of disgust toward all sexual matters and who had a history of overt homosexual experience. Among the abnormal women this group also re-ported a greater incidence of trauma following heterosexual experience, but this was not true of the normals.

The data cited in these three studies relate to sex aggres-sions, of course, and it is impossible to use them as an ade-quate check on Freud's theories, since he referred to the effects of other kinds of stimulation as well. There is no in-formation concerning perversions, and that relating to neu-rosis is inadequate. The general picture from the Hamilton and the Landis *et al.* studies is that sex aggressions are related to later sex difficulties; Terman's data do not support this and his sample was much more substantial and representative of the total population. In all probability some children do have their future sex activity distorted by such experiences. Others evidently do not.

Data relating to overstimulation are of a different charac-ter, though equally meager. Mead (1935), in her analysis of factors influencing the Arapesh personality, noted that oral stimulation was far more prevalent during the first four years than it is in most cultures. The child is given the breast re-peatedly, continuously, at every slight indication of hunger, injury or loneliness. The breast is used constantly as a re-ward and a restitution of rights and privileges. "From the time the little child is old enough to play with her breasts, the mother takes an active part in the suckling process. She holds her breast in her hand and gently vibrates the nipple inside the child's lips" (Mead, 1935, p. 42). Other forms of cutaneous stimulation occur but with less frequency than sucking. The child is gradually, and with difficulty, weaned between three and five and thereafter uses his fingers to stimulate his lips. This lip-play of the weaned child is interesting: "It flicks its upper lip with its thumb, with its first finger, with its second finger; it blows out its cheeks and pounds them; it bubbles its lips with the palm of its hand, with the back of its hand; it tickles the inside of its lower lip with its tongue; it licks its arms and its knees. A hundred different stylized ways of playing with the mouth are present in the play of the older children and gradually transmitted to the developing child." 2073701

This oral activity is certainly more common and pervasive than that of American children. The adult Arapesh also have such stimulation in the form of betel-chewing and smoking, which supersede the lip-play of childhood after initiation.

The effect of the orality on genitality is not clear. Mead describes the adult behavior as being lacking in genital-stimulated behavior and allocates all sex behavior to the marital relationship.

Malinowski (1927) has given an example of a culture in which genital sexuality is permitted as a form of play between boys and girls from infancy through adolescence. Actual penetration probably does not occur before 6 to 8 years of age in the girl and 10 to 12 in the boy but is common thereafter. These people, the Trobriand Islanders, are highly sexualized in their intersexual social relationships through adolescence. There is virtually complete promiscuity, but orgiastic behavior, exhibitionism, or other deviations from simple genital heterosexuality are not observed. Even in childhood, to say nothing of adolescence, sex play and intercourse are considered matters demanding privacy. This lack of unusual behavior, at least in any ritualized or obvious form, suggests that Freud's notions about the relation of perversion to over-stimulation in infancy are incorrect. The extensive genital sexuality of adolescence, however, is similar to the extensive orality of the Arapesh, and these two studies suggest that Freud may have been correct in supposing that overstimula-tion leads to a later domination of behavior by the drive com-ponent involved. One caution must be observed in this rea-soning, however; the Trobriand Islanders and the Arapesh are quite different peoples and it could conceivably be that genitality is more than usually vigorous in the former and orality is the same in the latter. In such case the early be-havior might be no more than a reflection of the same per-sistent internal pressure toward gratification that the later behavior is.

CONCLUSIONS

Both genital and pregenital behavior are socially oriented in many children. The fact that they are not more prominent-ly displayed is probably a function of social restriction, since observations of primitive peoples indicate the child's poten-tiality for elaborate and extensive enjoyment of such activity. There is, too, some slight cross-cultural evidence to give tenta-tive support to the theory that overstimulation of organic zones in childhood leads to overactivity of the congruent pleasure-seeking activity in adolescence.

Several sources of evidence indicate, however, that Freud seriously overestimated the frequency of the castration com-plex and the importance of childhood sex aggressions. The castration complex, like theories of the origin of babies, is a function of the kinds of information children have. Freud's tendency to rely on cultural universals—which do not exist—has led him to postulate universal attitudes and complexes that can be demonstrated in but a part of the population.

The influence of sex aggression is not universal, either; but the prevalence of perversions, neurosis and morbid prepossession with sexual matters that Freud attributed to such experiences can be accounted for differently. These experiences are outlawed in our own culture and the child who has them, either willingly or unwillingly, is made to feel guilty or ashamed; at the very least he knows he must not let his participation become public knowledge. Two consequences arise in this situation: first, he seeks new methods for achieving gratification. Other forbidden activities may be suggested to him by other children and these will automatically be associated with forbidden sexual behavior. His interest aroused, he will seek opportunities for sexual encounters and this will produce many of the infantile perversions. Second, the guilt and anxiety may in some instance lead to actual neurotic symptom formation. This would naturally be attributed to the experienced *event* rather than to the *emotions* involved. In adult recall, therefore, the cause of the neurosis might seem limited to the sexual experience, whereas in truth it lay in a complicated relationship in which the sexual experience was a more or less fortuitous excitant.

Chapter III

Object Choice

THE GENERAL OUTLINES of Freud's theory of object choice or cathexis, as described in the second and third of the *Three Contributions,* can be set forth briefly. Genital sexuality in the infant is not in any sense fully developed as to object, and what concentration of libidinal energy there may be in that zone is at first limited in its effect to autoerotic behavior. Infantile masturbation is essentially narcissistic. However, from the first the child is treated to much affection and erogenous stimulation by the mother, and hence he gradually develops a well-organized sexual attachment to her. By the age of five this is strongly developed. The form of this genital behavior is necessarily different from that of the adult because of the immaturity of his infantile sexual apparatus. In the boy, the parental attachment is broken at six to eight years, sometimes by threats of castration (Freud, 1924), and the latency period begins, to be followed later by a choice of new objects, some of them homosexual and some heterosexual. The latter type of object is preponderant in adolescence, however, because the initial attachments of childhood were heterosexual and these objects now have greater value. In the girl, the initial attachment to the mother gives way to a love for the father, which is less subject to interruption than is the Oedipus relationship in the boy. (Freud, 1933)

There are possible sources of pathology in this sequence, however, and the sexual inhibitions associated with adult neurosis arise from the too powerful inhibiting of sexual attachment to the cross-sex parent in the second half of child-hood. The increase in strength of sexual impulse at adolescence increases the conflict over expression of the impulses, and hysteria may result (Fenichel, 1934, p. 18).

The details of this process vary from one person to another, especially with reference to the nature of the earliest object cathexes and the techniques by which they are broken, but the general pattern is said to be constant. As will be seen below, there is support for both contentions; there are enormous individual variations in sexual development, but in some persons at least, the descriptive aspects of the picture follow roughly along the lines Freud has described.

THE SELF AS OBJECT

The data relating to choice of sex objects in early infancy are of minimal significance. The observations of Halverson have shown that genital excitation occurs from birth, but there are no data of a directly observational sort that indicate the nature of any infantile object attachments involving actual genital excitation.

1. *Narcissism.* Evidence as to narcissistic cathexis (Freud, 1914) during this period is equally unsatisfactory. The concept itself does not allow of a positive definition; it can be recognized in behavior only as a nonattachment to other persons. Since children gradually begin to show affection toward parents, siblings and other children from the age of a few months, it may be supposed that the narcissism (if any) gradually gives way to object cathexes. Hamilton (1929, p. 465) found that only 2 of his men and 3 of his women could recall taking pleasure in the sight or feel of their own bodies during childhood. Since two thirds of the hundred men and half the hundred women acknowledged having had such feelings at some time during their lives, these childhood recollec-

tions may merely have been displaced in time. It is doubtful, in any case, whether such feelings could be recalled from the first year or two of life. The question was designed to secure reference to a kind of behavior or reaction that is more characteristic of sensitive and highly verbal adults than of preverbal infants.

2. *Masturbation*. The autoerotism of genital masturbation has already been described in the previous chapter. The age of onset may be as early as the first few months, and Levy (1928) reports a high incidence in boys during the first 18 months. These data are of limited value because of their source—parental recall of casual observation—but may reasonably be considered as giving a minimal frequency.

The course of autoerotic practices during infancy, childhood and adolescence is not at all clear. Willoughby's excellent summary of the literature (1937) includes no observational studies, but the abundance of data based on adult recall gives one a fair degree of confidence in the findings so far as later childhood is concerned. These papers indicate that on the average about 5 per cent of men and 18 per cent of women had begun masturbation before 10 years of age. These figures must be reconciled with Levy's report that genital manipulation had been observed by 3 years in 53 per cent of the 49 boys whose mothers he questioned. The reconcilement is not hard; the behavior described as "masturbation" during adolescence is obviously quite different from "observed genital manipulation" in the infant. The former represents habitual action and the latter might be reported if of but occasional occurrence.

Whatever may be the case with reference to the first decade, Willoughby has shown that there is a sharp increase in frequency at the onset of adolescence in boys; the increase with girls is more gradual and the frequency never attains the height that it does in boys, although it starts higher at age 10.

Freud's theoretical formulation of the three stages of masturbation, infantile, pre-Oedipal, and pubertal, is too vague to permit of detailed validation. In general, the facts indicate that masturbation in infancy is fairly common and that there is a large increase during puberty; but there are no data to show whether during later childhood habitual self-manipulation actually decreases in a particular child. Davis (1929) has given ample evidence that, within a *group of girls,* initial *recalled* onset increases in frequency of report through age 8 and does not diminish until adolescence.

The lack of consistent drops or increments in frequency of reported onset suggests that Freud's rather elaborate schematization of the masturbation sequence does not reflect the facts in any general way, whatever may be its cogency with reference to some individual cases.

THE OEDIPUS SITUATION

Contemporary views of the parent-child relationship seem to depend historically on Freud's description of the Oedipus situation. In the ensuing thirty-five years other influences and sources of data have been brought to bear on the problem, however, and today it is difficult to summarize the findings unless one limits the discussion rigidly to Freud's own rather narrow conception of the Oedipus situation and its consequences. The more realistic approach, assimilating the modern emphasis on the family as a social unit and utilizing the data of child guidance clinics, has already been taken by Symonds (1939), whose important review needs no supplement for the present.

The Oedipus situation (Freud, 1920, pp. 285-293; 1924), the sexual attachment of a child for the cross-sex parent, develops originally as a result of the mother's stimulation of the child and her giving of gratification through feeding, bathing, etc.; in this way the child passes from autoerotism to object cathexis. The continuation of this relationship eventuates in an actual genital love response. This is furthered by the mother's inevitable discriminative reaction to the boy as an opposite-sex person and the father's same response to the girl. Correlated with these relationships are the antagonisms for the parent of the same sex.

1. *Parent preferences.* Any effort to obtain the facts about these relationships at once runs into the snag of definition. What is an "attachment"? Is it any degree of affection at all or does it imply a deeper and more pervasive connection? In an effort to discover something about the strength of parent-child attachments, Terman (1938) had his subjects in the marriage study rate, on a 5-point scale, both attachment to and conflict with each parent. Contrary to the Freudian theory, he found that there was little or no difference between the sexes in the amount of attachment to each parent, and that in both cases it was greater with the mother. The ratings on amount of interpersonal conflict indicate somewhat less between boys and their mothers than between boys and their fathers; there is a very slight tendency of the opposite sort with girls. In all cases the differences are too small to be of great import. Taking the population as a whole, there is no support for the theory that the cross-sex parent is favored and that powerful jealousy reactions are developed toward the same-sex parent.

These results corroborate a number of studies cited by Stogdill (1937), who has reviewed the quantitative literature to 1936. In no instance has a reliable difference between boys and girls been found as to preference for either parent. These are group facts, however, not relevant to the individual child and it must be emphasized that non-analytic research gives information most often about tendencies in total populations, not absolute relationships within single cases.

After adolescence the same situation holds true. Stagner and Drought (1935) constructed attitude scales for measuring degree of affection toward each parent. Neither men nor women college students showed a difference between the parents. It is interesting to note, however, that the two scales correlated only +.16, which would seem to indicate that individual persons were not customarily equal in their affection for both parents.

Terman's results with reference to interpersonal conflict are supported by Stott (1940), who secured free criticisms of both parents from nearly a thousand adolescents of both sexes, derived about equally from farms, small towns and a large city. Girls were definitely more critical of both parents than were the boys but there was no difference between the parents. Stott's method was to ask, simply, what there was about each parent that was criticizable. The score was in terms of presence or absence of an answer. It is possible that the girls, being more verbal and "literary," might have been more critical merely by being more cooperative and conscientious in answering the questionnaire.

In the more revealing discussions of their early emotions, Hamilton's 200 subjects described many rather unique and complicated intrafamilial relationships. The details cannot be conveniently summarized but these data again argue against any universal pattern and reemphasize the point that obtrudes itself time and again in the examination of such studies as these—that the structure of the little societies in which people grow up are too varied as to detail ever to permit of the kinds of generalizations that Freud has made concerning the role of specific members of the family.

2. *Other heterosexual cathexes.* The implication of the

Oedipus interpretation of affection during the late infancy period is that this is the primary source of heterosexual object choice. The early study of Bell (1902), however, showed that powerful and dominating heterosexual attachments between children occur as early as two years. Bell secured observational reports of juvenile love affairs from several hundred teachers; also "confessions" of their own. These freely described cases (of which there were about 1700), in addition to 800 affairs observed by Bell himself, composed the data from which some rather significant conclusions were drawn. Unhappily the data are not presented in statistical detail but only as a multitude of illustrative case examples.

Bell found that the love affairs of the children were in some instances highly sexualized and produced the physiological signs of sex excitation. This was not the usual experience, but in all other respects such as methods of courtship, tenderness, protectiveness, masculine exhibitionism, feminine coyness, hugging, kissing and shyness the affairs were little different from those of adults. Bell found it possible to distinguish the infantile, latency and adolescent periods that Freud was later to describe, and was able to give a considerably more factual and realistic account of the early sex behavior than Freud ever gave. Bell limited his interest to heterosexual attachments between contemporaries, however; there are no data on incestuous or homosexual relationships.

This study, with its emphasis on the strength of early attachments *outside the family,* must necessarily cast doubt on the alleged universality of the Oedipus situation. The latter's chief importance in the psychoanalytic theory is, first, as a pattern that is laid down early and thereafter serves either as the archetype or as the source of anxiety for all future love relations. Bell's findings suggest that there may be other sources of equal significance. The second important aspect of the Oedipus situation is its repression at ages 6 to 8, and Bell's data show that this is not characteristic of all these extra-familial relationships; many of them are reported to have continued to adolescence or adulthood and some even to have eventuated in marriage. There are no data available to clarify the relation between these juvenile affairs and parental attachments.

LATENCY PERIOD

One consequence of the suppression of the Oedipus situation is the elimination of a sexual object during the period of later childhood (Freud, 1905, p. 59). During this time the child is more or less desexualized, according to the theory.

The validity of this proposition varies directly with the culture to which it is applied. Malinowski (1927) found no evidence among the Trobriand Islanders for such a letdown in genital sexuality; indeed, the sex play became increasingly direct and its cultural control more highly formalized. In Middle Western United States, on the other hand, Bell found a marked change associated with the years 6 to 12. The typical pattern was one of shyness and avoidance of overt contact with the heterosexual love object in nonformalized context. Under more ritualized conditions, however, such as in kissing and hugging game, the contacts so characteristic of earlier years continued. In no sense could it be said that the youngster was objectless, and even in the staid confines of the Victorian parlor the game of "Post Office" suggested a sexual undercurrent in the playful contacts.

A more detailed and probably more accurate picture of the social sexual behavior from 5 to 16 has been achieved by Campbell (1939) in her observational study of 46 boys and 39 girls enrolled in the Merrill-Palmer clubs. This group was studied for three years by means of continuous observation of social behavior units. From these units, properly allocated as to age, "social-sex" maturity scales were formed for both boys and girls. Some sample items, from the boys' scale, together with the ages for which they are characteristic, will indicate the kinds of behavior to which the scales apply.

> 6.0 Will play in a group composed entirely of girls because not yet sex-conscious
> 8.0 Does not differentiate work according to sex
> 9.5 Plays pursuit games in fun with girls
> 12.0 Will touch girls only in games or other conventionalized situations
> 14.5 Attempts to improve his personal appearance in order to attract girls

All the 46 items of the boys' scale and the 48 of the girls' are not as objective as these, and it is clear from Campbell's description of her technique of choice that only extensive acquaintance with a child will permit a rating for him; the scale is not designed for short sample observations.

It is perfectly clear that the kinds of behavior here described are a function of the immediate social milieu and that different groups would progress at different rates and, possibly, with some parts of the sequence inverted. For this one group, however, it is equally clear that the sequence did not contain any sharp break at 6 to 8 years or at the beginning of puberty. Instead, there appears to have been a gradual development of sex-consciousness between 9.0 and 11.0 years. This led at first to a rejection and avoidance of the opposite sex, then shy acceptance, and finally to wholehearted seeking of physical and social contact. The onset of these changes in object of sex regard came considerably before puberty and fell definitely in the latency period. These figures represent "norms" rather than exactly calculated averages, and no measures of dispersion are available.

The reports by Achilles (1923), and Davis (1929), and Hamilton (1929) of romantic love affairs and heterosexual play during this period are generally substantiated in the other sources cited by Willoughby (1937). There are no data available, however, to indicate whether the relatively smaller amount of object-directed sexual behavior in American and European children than in certain primitive groups is a function of the suppression of the Oedipus reaction or whether it is a function of increased efforts at nonsexual socialization, partly through formalized schooling and partly through specific control by authority of sex behavior. One would be bold to assume that either factor alone was the sole agent in all children, although it may be supposed that in some few individuals the spread of inhibition from Oedipus suppression might be predominant. This may have been characteristic of the neurotic persons from whom Freud obtained his evidently erroneous conception of the latency period.

HOMOSEXUALITY

1. *Oedipus influence.* Freud suggested two sources of homosexuality, one of which is a definite consequence of the Oedipus situation. According to this reasoning (1905, p. 10, footnote 12), the strong suppression of (a boy's) affection for the mother by punishment could create an inhibition of reactiveness to females in general, and, under the heightened genital excitation at puberty, he would seek men as sexual partners to avoid the anxiety induced by sexual impulses toward women. The same relationship could hold true with women.

The evidence is clear that homosexual behavior is common both before and immediately after the onset of puberty. In Hamilton's group the frequency of various types of genital play was approximately the same between 6 and 11 as between 12 and 15. This was true of both boys and girls. This prepubertal homoerotism would to some extent coincide with the rejection of heterosexual partners described by Campbell, but data are not available to show individual relationships. With the demonstration that genital impulses are common during the years from 9 to 12, this prepubertal homoerotism can be considered affirmative to Freud's theory; it must represent simply another form of rejection of heterosexuality. There is nothing compelling either logically or factually, however, about this affirmation.

A more important kind of evidence relates to the connection between intrafamilial attachments and homoerotism. Hamilton (pp. 500-501) secured fairly detailed recalls of his subjects' emotional reactions to their parents and siblings. Truly incestuous sexual feelings were reported by 54 men and 29 women as having occurred at some time in their early lives, but 28 of these men acknowledged such feelings as relating to sisters only and 15 of the women connected them with brothers or other nonpaternal males (pp. 484-485). The remainder had either parents or parents and siblings as objects. However, for purposes of discovering the influence of incestuous feelings on later sexual reactivity, Hamilton grouped parent and sibling incest feelings together. A comparison of the two groups, one able and the other unable to recall incestuous feelings, showed that such feelings were definitely correlated in men with recall of "significant friendships" (probably homoerotic), mutual sex organ stimulation with childhood friends of either or both sexes, and definite homosexual experiences after the 18th year. The first two relationships are highly reliable, the latter one considerably less so. In women, only the first relationship is statistically significant. In both sexes, however, the frequencies indicate that many who had had homoerotic feelings did not recall incestuous ones and vice versa.

Landis *et al.* (pp. 311-312) secured a measure of attachment to family by careful analysis of the interview data from their women subjects. By comparison of those who appeared to be *tied to the family* with those who did not, this attachment was found to be reliably associated with a general lack of outgoing or object-directed sexuality. As adults these closely tied women lacked interest in sex and had no reportable sex feelings. They were usually virgins at marriage or, in the case of the single women interviewed, at the time of the study. They had had fewer than average love affairs with men and more often than not acknowledged frequent or even excessive masturbation. The fact that they also had suffered poorer health than the average in childhood suggests that the attachment may have been caused by that and not necessarily by overstimulation of sexual love. The possibility can not be ignored that the poor health in childhood may itself have been an indicator of repression of sexuality in some cases, but this is purely speculative.

A comparison of those 73 who had some homoerotic trend, including 8 overt homosexuals, with the 222 who showed no such tendencies, indicated that the former had, with markedly greater frequency, been fonder of one parent than the other both in childhood and during the teens. The father and mother are not separated in the data. The homoerotic also more frequently had a history of childhood sexual experience or aggression and frequent or excessive masturbation. They also reported resentment at the social restrictions involved in being a woman, a characteristic that Freud suggested would follow from the masculine identification in late infancy. This picture is moderately faithful to that to be expected from the Freudian theory, but again it must be remembered that this is a composite picture, not an individual one.

2. *Hamilton's syndrome.* The logical possibility remains,

however, that there may be a characteristic consequence of the Oedipus situation, and that this may be a constellation of behavior forms of sufficient fixity to be called a syndrome. Freud suggested the possibility that such an outcome might be a function of some unspecified aspect of the sexual constitution.

By a pattern analysis of his data, Hamilton (p. 526) discovered 4 women who might be considered "classical" Oedipus cases. In their childhood they had been unusually fond of their fathers and jealous of their mothers. The father was described as having especially attractive physical features, and the daughter was always on affectionate terms with him; she was not demonstrative toward the mother, however, and was not on friendly terms with her. In addition there was a history of inadequate preparation for menstruation and general lack of opportunity for sex information. There were remembered episodes of childhood nastiness.

From this background came, in the adult, a curiously deviant pattern of sexuality. These women were homoerotic and autoerotic; masturbation continued after marriage and they were definitely narcissistic at a physical level. They had sexual daydreams. They were heterosexually promiscuous both before and after marriage and complained that their husbands were unattractive as sex partners, that the sex act was unpleasant to them, that their orgasm capacity was inadequate, and that their marriages were unhappy. They also reported a history of fearing that they were physically unattractive to men.

An almost identical picture of 8 homosexual women is given by Henry and Galbraith (1934). These had all had heterosexual intercourse and 7 of the 8 were promiscuous; the eighth left her husband five weeks after marriage. Six of them had masturbated in childhood and continued to gain sexual gratification that way. All were frigid in their hetero-sexual relations. All had a history of prepubertal masturba-tion and recalled episodes of sexual aggression in childhood.

Included in the Landis study were 8 women who acknowl-edged overt homoerotism and, of these, 6 reported prepuber-tal sex aggression and 5 of them had had complete sex experi-ence. Their affectional relations to parents were not reported.

These various behavior items occur independently in large numbers of women and the data do not reveal whether there is a continuous distribution of cases between "presence of all" and "presence of none" of the items. If so there is no reason for considering this a syndrome, but if a relatively small num-ber of cases pile up at the "all" end, then it may be some aspect of the early sex experience has had a characteristic reactive value. This seems a possible interpretation.

3. *Associative homosexuality.* The second source of homo-sexuality that Freud described was continued association with same-sex persons during childhood (1905, p. 86). When a child gains gratification from a person of the same sex, he chooses that sex preferentially later. Since the norm is for both sexes to be reared primarily by women, it would be expected that boys would usually be heterosexual but that girls would show a relatively greater tendency toward homosexuality.

The validity of the last point, involving a comparison be-tween the sexes, is doubtful. Only two studies have asked the questions about homosexuality of both sexes in the same way, thus making the percentage results for the two sexes com-parable. Hamilton (p. 497) found that 17 men and 26 women had had homosexual play episodes since the 18th year, but other questions relating to imagining and feeling revealed a confused picture of relative frequency. Terman (p. 341) se-cured ratings of strength of homosexual impulses on a 4-point scale for both husbands and wives about both self and spouse.

The women show a slightly greater frequency, but the differences are minimal.

As Terman points out, inversion is more acceptable among women and popularly believed to be more common. This could conduce to a larger frequency of positive replies, since the anxiety engendered by such admission would be less for the women than for men.

An opposite argument can equally well be presented by reference to the process of identification. The child identifies himself with the adults who have given him gratification. He adopts their attitudes, beliefs, mannerisms, ideals and goals. If a boy is reared by women only, if he has no opportunity to absorb masculinity from his environment, he might be expected as an adult to be feminine in behavior and to adopt the feminine role in social and sexual relationships. He might, in other words, become a passive homosexual.

Some evidence obtained by Terman and Miles (1936) supports this hypothesis. In 18 case histories of passive male homosexuals there is a clear trend of close attachment to the mother in early childhood and an avoidance of the father. In 15 of the 18 cases, the father died when the subject was young, was away from home most of the time or was described as "cold, stern, autocratic or fear-inspiring." Only 3 of the fathers were described as sympathetic and none was the preferred parent. This proportion is quite different from that obtained by Terman (1938, p. 218) in his study of marriage. In that group of 728 married men, 43 per cent said there was no difference in the strength of their attachment to father and to mother and an additional 13 per cent had a stronger attachment to the father. These control data are not entirely satisfactory, since the ratings of attachment were secured in such a different way from the data concerning the homosexual group; but what evidence there is does appear to support the expectation that intimate and prolonged preferential association with the mother leads to passive homosexuality of the son.

Terman and Miles (p. 224) give other data, however, that confuse this picture somewhat. They secured scores on their masculinity-femininity test of 25 men who had been under the care of their mothers either altogether or most of the time up to age 12. A comparison of these with the scores of the comparably educated group of 344 males from which this subgroup was taken showed that the former had, on the average, reliably more masculine scores. The M-F test measures interests and attitudes that have been shown empirically to differentiate the sexes. These data make it appear that boys brought up in close association with the mother develop more than average masculine interests and attitudes. This finding is particularly striking in view of the fact that a group of 77 passive male homosexuals (from which the 18 case histories were drawn) had an average M-F score but little more masculine than that of high school girls.

Thus it appears that the case histories of passive male homosexuals support the prediction, but the M-F scores of those men whose experiences should theoretically lead them to become homosexual are the very opposite of those of a group of known homosexuals.

These same relationships do not apply to women. Those brought up only or chiefy under the care of either the father or the mother proved to be no more feminine (or masculine) than the average of the total group. A group of 18 female homosexuals, some active and some passive, had an average M-F score reliably more masculine than that of a group of equivalent professional women, however. It is evident that no final conclusion as to the validity of Freud's suggestion can be reached from these data, but the constancy of a strong mother attachment in the passive male homosexual case histories reflects the same kind of clinical observation that Freud made.

THE MARITAL PARTNER

The general principle applied above to the determination of homo- or heterosexuality of object choice can be applied to the problem of choice of spouse also. If the early experiences of heterosexual love are of great influence in determining later choice, there ought to be a measurable resemblance between the spouse and the opposite-sex parent.

In an attempt to test this conclusion, Commins (1932) sought to discover the age at which men in different ordinal positions marry. He reasoned that the mother of a first son is on the average younger than the mother of later born ones and that the first born would therefore marry earlier. Commins secured data from the English "Who's Who" and made the necessary comparison, finding that oldest sons married younger than nonoldest. But as Commins recognized himself, there are uncontrolled factors of economics and primogeniture that invalidate the results.

A different technique for checking this same point was used by Kirkpatrick (1937), who correlated the age of mother at boy's birth with *relative age* of girl he married. A coefficient of $+.03$ was secured, but the interpretation of the second of the two variables measured is not entirely clear.

An altogether different approach to the problem was made by Mangus (1936), whose subjects were nearly 600 upperclass women college students, mostly unmarried. He limited his consideration to the conception of an *ideal* husband, and determined the degree of similarity between this conception and the described personalities of three males: father, most intimate other male relative, and most intimate nonrelated male companion. The data from which the comparisons were made were rather elaborate paired comparisons of social roles and personality traits. By applying contingency measures to the 26 separate items used in each of the 4 different descriptions, Mangus was led to the conclusion that the *ideal* of a husband was more similar to the father with respect to social role but more similar to the most intimate nonrelated male companion with respect to personality traits.

The results do not bear directly on the question of the relation between husband and father and it might well be that the male companion influenced the husband ratings but that marriage would actually occur only when the father's image could be matched. No information is available as to the relation between such *ideals* and the personality of the flesh and blood man later chosen.

The various data relating to the problem are inadequate for purposes of verification of the hypothesis.

EXPERIMENTAL CONTROL OF CATHEXIS

Without going into detail about the process of cathexis, Freud suggested that the love reaction was produced by gratification; the mother was loved by the child because she fulfilled its wants. But because experimentalists have been concerned about hedonic attributes of objects largely in terms of the hedonic quality itself, and have studied gratification chiefly with respect to its influence on learning, there are few data relevant to cathexis.

Several demonstrations of Freud's general principle have been reported, however; the sources of gratifications have been two, success at competitive activities and "identification with loved objects." The former, success, was ingeniously utilized by Mierke (1933) in a laboratory experiment with school children. He had them perform a number of difficult construction tasks with small colored sticks. The sticks were of several different colors and each child was allowed to state his preferences as to colors in advance. During the actual construction tests success was permitted with nonpreferred colors and failure was artificially introduced with preferred colors. In an elaborate determination of color preferences afterward, it was discovered that the preferences had been reversed. Somewhat similar results were obtained by Rosenzweig (1937) and H. H. Nowlis (1941) in other experiments involving success and failure.

These studies indicate clearly that preference or liking, which can be looked at as rather emasculated instances of cathexis, occurs when the objects are instrumental to gratification. This is hardly a novel outcome, but the excellent experimental techniques of these studies should be applicable to more extensive analyses of such problems as generalization of cathexis and identification with cathected objects.

The generalization of cathexis through identification with the hero of a story has also been studied. Duncker (1938) reported a reversal of children's food preferences following the reading of an animal story in which the mouse hero indicated a decided preference for the food previously unpreferred by the children. In contrast to this method of having the child actually demonstrate his new-found liking is the method of verbal attitude scale measurement employed by Thurstone (1931a, 1931b) and Peterson and Thurstone (1932), who showed pictures with highly dramatic content to groups of school children. Some involved Chinese and Germans as heroes. By using carefully constructed attitude scales before and after the pictures, the investigators were able to show that there was an increase in favorableness of attitude toward the nationality of the characters with whom the audience identified. Generalization of cathexis can occur, therefore, beyond the original person or object through whom, by identification, gratification has been secured. The limiting conditions, duration and nonverbal consequences of this process need exploration. Motion pictures might prove a highly useful medium for such research if the task of securing appropriate films did not prove impossible.

The general problem of cathexis is an extremely important one. Psychoanalysis has relied heavily on the disposition of positive and negative affects as an explanation of much of human behavior. Such concepts as libido and ambivalence, and such critical complications as the Oedipus complex, are directly dependent on the manner and direction of cathexes. Without further understanding of the mechanics of the process itself, the very fundamentals of the whole system lie in darkness. The data cited here represent nothing but goads to further research.

CONCLUSIONS

One conclusion stands out above all others: emotional development, as couched in terms of successive object choices, is far more variable than Freud supposed. This is not to say that none of the classical elements appears. They do; but with too many exceptions to be accepted as typical. The conditions under which object choice is made explain why this is. Object choice is essentially a function of learning and what is learned is a function of the environment in which the learning occurs. Since there is no universal culture pattern for intrafamilial relationships, there can be no universal pattern of learned object choices.

In spite of the variability of the developmental process, there are certain points at which Freud's skilled clinical observation provided generalizations that are largely supported by later and more objective observations. The autoerotism of infancy, the early childhood development of heterosexual object cathexes, the associative source of some cases of homosexuality, and the origin of cathexis in gratification are seen by other investigators in much the same light as they were seen by Freud. The rigid Oedipus relationship and the latency period, however, appear to be too dependent on specific conditions of learning to be demonstrable in large populations. The fact that the father and cross-sex siblings are among the important love objects of both boys and girls may be a reflection of a difference in the cultural milieus of the populations that Freud observed and those subjected to study by other investigators.

Chapter IV

Distortions of Sexuality

UNLIKE HIS THEORIES of infantile sexuality and the Oedipus situation, Freud's suggestions about the antecedents of sexual pathology have no implications of universality. The psychoanalytic literature is rich in hypotheses as to the sources of these disorders and it is a great misfortune that the data for further analysis and verification are so scanty. It is here, where clinical insights may reveal enormous areas of understandable behavior, that Freud's theories should be examined by other techniques. The notions relating to a universal psychosexual structure have two strikes against them already—they are derived from the few neurotics rather than from the many normals and they deal with factors that depend on cultural universals, of which there are none. But the syndromes, the pathological sequences, the unique mechanics of distortion, these are the things Freud had direct experience of and it is here we should expect validation by further investigation.

HYPOSEXUALITY

1. *Orgasm inadequacy*. Freud discussed this form of female frigidity in general terms only, but Fenichel (1934, p. 110) has summarized the gradual accretion of psychoanalytic theories of its sources. These can be summarized as follows: 1) inhibition of sexuality resulting from fears induced during infancy, 2) infantile fixation of sexuality on the clitoris, 3) masculine identification leading to a failure to combine sexuality with the normal feminine masochism.

Direct investigation of these hypotheses would be impossible except by psychoanalysis itself, and it is therefore necessary to search for behavioral correlates of these processes.

The association of anxiety and guilt with genital sexuality can be measured in either of two ways: by searching the life history for antecedents that should cause them, and by discovering overt manifestations of them in adult sex behavior. Fortunately we can do both. The studies of marriage by Hamilton (1929) and Terman (1938) have included a considerable amount of data that both authors have applied to the problem of orgasm adequacy. Each has divided his total group of women subjects into the "adequates" and "inadequates" and has compared the frequency of various possible correlates in the two groups. It is possible, therefore, to select a number of items which have theoretical relevance and check with these two investigations as to the degree of relationship.

The occurrence of childhood sex aggressions or shock might be supposed to create anxiety and fear of sexual activities; Hamilton found a reliable association of such experience with inadequacy, but Terman did not. It is hard to evaluate such a disagreement. Hamilton had 54 adequates and 46 inadequates; Terman had approximately 500 and 250 respectively. The size of sample favors Terman's findings, but the intensity of investigation favors Hamilton's.

No such discrepancy occurs with reference to the "goodness" of sex instruction. Hamilton had 4 items relating to this matter and 2 of these gave a positive relation between non-anxiety-provoking sources and orgasm adequacy. The other 2 items showed no difference between the groups. Terman had 3 items and all showed a definitely positive relation.

Terman had 3 items relating to childhood happiness, which might conceivably relate to presence of infantile anxieties, but all 3 showed a complete lack of relationship.

The painfulness or shocking character of the first experience of intercourse would be another possible source of
anxiety even though it did not occur in childhood. Hamilton
had 2 items that measured this but neither discriminated reliably between the groups. Terman had 2 items also, but
only 1 discriminated; it was positive, however.

The Oedipus situation, when it exists as a strongly emotional factor in the girl's life, would naturally produce
anxiety about sexual impulses. Hamilton found evidence that
such was the case but the differences are not great and there
were several exceptions. Terman had 5 items that related to
the early attachments to and conflicts with the parents, but
none of the differences was favorable to the hypothesis and
2 were small but negative to it.

So far as the type of reaction to sex stimulation in adulthood is concerned, Hamilton found a slight tendency for
girls who reacted to their first arousal of desire with anxiety
to have less orgasm adequacy. Terman found, however, that
those who looked forward to sex experience in marriage with
pleasant anticipation were no more likely to have adequate
orgasms than those who looked forward to it with disgust or
indifference. An attitude of "passionate longing" favored adequacy to a very slight degree.

These findings do not support the anxiety and guilt interpretation very strongly.

The second hypothesis, relating to infantile fixation on the
clitoris, is virtually impossible to test by other than the analytic data themselves. If fixation is interpreted in terms of habit,
i.e., as an unusually strong habit, it might be further deduced
that masturbation would be commoner among those with
inadequate orgasm. Hamilton (pp. 441-442) was able to divide
his 100 women subjects into 3 groups with reference to masturbation, those who denied it as a postmarital activity (44

cases), those who did it rarely (45 cases), and those who did it with considerable frequency (11 cases). There was no difference between the first two groups, but only 3 of the 11 women in the last one were adequate. Because of the extremely small number of cases involved, this represents only a tentative support for the deduction. Hamilton also noted, however, that of the 64 women who acknowledged masturbation at some time in their lives, only 8 said sexual daydreams were an essential aspect of the masturbation and all of these were adequates. The frequency of adequates among the remaining 58 women was less (45 per cent) than among the total group (54 per cent). If the lack of imagery indicated a purely autoerotic gratification from the clitoris, this difference might also be said to support the deduction.

There are no data with which to test the third hypothesis.

2. *Lack of sex drive.* Although a number of interesting correlates of psychosexual and sociosexual immaturity have been discovered by Terman and by Landis, the lack of sex drive is generally considered to be a symptom deriving from too many different sources to permit of the testing of any one by the quantitative data.

HYPERSEXUALITY AND PERVERSION

The source of hypersexuality lies in undischarged pregenital tensions, according to Fenichel (1934, p. 290), and the uncontrolled behavior is an attempt to relieve them. An underlying sadistic trend is also associated with it. This, taken in conjunction with Freud's statements (1905, p. 30) that each perverted impulse is accompanied by its opposite and that there is a correlation among all the perverted impulses, suggests that any group exhibiting one of the deviations in sex object or sex aim would, in comparison with a nondeviant group, display more of the others also.

The incidence of the various component "perversions" of which Freud spoke proved to be surprisingly high in the group studied by Hamilton (pp. 446-466). Table 3 gives the

TABLE 3. Number of Hamilton's subjects who reported "perverse" behavior at some time during their lives. (From Hamilton, 1929, pp. 448–465)

Behavior	No. of Subjects		Hamilton's Table No.
	Men (N = 100)	Women (N = 100)	
Anal erotism	34	15	386
Urethral erotism	37	20	387
Exhibitionism			
Childhood	53	25	389
Postpuberty	34	22	394
Voyeurism: impulse	89	58	400
Sadism	51	32	408
Masochism	24	29	411
Fetichism	59	49	414
Narcissism	64	55	419

frequency with which each kind was reported by both men and women. Also worth noting is the fact that, at the time of the interviews, 26 men and 16 women still had exhibitionistic impulses and 81 men and 15 women still had voyeuristic impulses. While the men were relatively more voyeuristic and the women more exhibitionistic, the men outdid the women in both instances.

A similar but even more striking sex difference existed with reference to sadism-masochism; men were more sadistic and women more masochistic. Masochism was the only perverse behavior more frequently reported by women than by men. At the time of the interview, 25 men and 16 women still had sadistic impulses, and 14 men and 25 women still had masochistic wishes. It appears that men are relatively more sadistic and women more masochistic. This verifies common clinical observation.

Since there were 100 men and 100 women in the study, the above figures are also per cents. An astonishingly large proportion of the group was able to recall having felt the existence of each of these "polymorphous perverse" impulses. This supports Freud's observation of the frequency (or even existence) of such motivation, but the ease with which so many of these normal adults were able to recall forbidden experiences is a little surprising in view of Freud's insistence that so much is hidden beneath infantile amnesia and can be recalled only through the arduous labor of psychoanalysis. (Cf. Chapter VI.)

Hamilton does not present the intercorrelations among these various perverse activities but his calculation of the frequency of adequate orgasm in women in relation to each of the kinds of perverseness indicates that without exception there is greater adequacy associated with a *lack* of such report of perversion. This is true of anal erotism, urethral erotism, exhibitionism, voyeurism, sadism, masochism, fetichism and narcissism. The differences are all relatively small but the cumulative reliability of 8 such comparisons is impressive. This appears to support, in an unexpected direction, the hypothesis of correlation among sexual deviations.

More extensive data are available with respect to hypersexuality. The Hamilton syndrome described in Chapter III is the extreme instance. In it are merged the autoerotic action and both homo- and heterosexuality. Landis *et al.* (pp. 311-312) found homoerotism associated to a reliable degree with frequent or excessive masturbation and the latter with an obsessive interest in sex. Bromley and Britten (1938), without giving exact figures, claim to have found that homosexual college men had more often been seriously troubled by masturbation than heterosexual men had been. Davis (1929), whose data on this matter are unusually complete, found that 18 of her 1000 married women had had overt homosexual experience after marriage. These women had had reliably more pre-adolescent sex play, masturbation at times not specified, and sexual intercourse before marriage. The discrepancy between the two groups was particularly large on the last item with respect to frequency of intercourse with others than fiancé. A comparison can be made in Davis' data, also, between overt and nonovert homosexuals as to frequency of masturbation practiced at some time. The former group had greater frequency.

These various findings sum up to this principle: any deviation from conventional heterosexual behavior is accompanied by a greater tendency to masturbation, homosexuality and promiscuous heterosexual activity. There are no data concerning the frequency of pregenital or perverse behavior in such cases.

Promiscuity is not the only criterion of hypersexuality, however. Frequency of intercourse by married couples can also be used. Both the social and psychological significance of the two criteria differ decidedly, but each relates to the gross frequency of sexual behavior. In order to study the correlates of *marital* hypersexuality, Terman selected a group of 65 "passionate" wives for comparison with a group of 81 "nonpassionate" wives. As a group the former averaged 12.6 copulations per month and expressed an average wish for 14.2 per month. The group of nonpassionate wives had an average copulatory frequency of 3.6 per month and average wish for only 1.8 per month.

Various other measures of sex behavior were found to be correlated with the copulatory measure of passionateness. Nearly twice as many of the P (passionate) wives were adequate as to orgasm and had a history of adequacy at first intercourse. The P group had a reliably greater number who rarely or never refused intercourse (to their husbands), only half as many who were virgins at marriage, twice as many who had had intercourse with their husbands before marriage, and half again as many who had had intercourse with others. Twice as many acknowledged that during adolescence they had "petted" frequently or very frequently, and more had had a premarital attitude toward sex of interest or passionate longing.

The childhood histories showed that the P wives almost twice as frequently had more than a moderate attachment to the father and rated the father above average in attractiveness. There was some tendency, too, for the husband to have a closer resemblance to the father than was the case with the N-P wives. There were no differences in amount of conflict with either parent but both groups were considerably higher than the total population of the investigation (N=782) on attachment to mother.

Two separate pictures of hypersexuality appear to resolve from these data. On the one hand there are the unhappy and seemingly tense women who have a history of masturbation and homosexual attachments and who have extensive heterosexual experience both before and after marriage. They find marriage unsatisfactory and fall in love with other men, but since this happens repeatedly it must be presumed that they are unable to make a really satisfactory sexual attachment. In spite of their apparent hypersexuality they are unable to have orgasm and they often refuse to have intercourse with their husbands.

The other picture of hypersexuality is that drawn by Terman. The "passionate" wives have a history of affectionate family life and early indications of strong heterosexual drive. Their marriages are somewhat happier than average; they do not desire extramarital intercourse more often than average; and they have relatively few complaints about their husbands as sexual partners.

The nature of the data from which these descriptions are taken does not permit us to discover what the true relationship is between these two kinds of women. Terman did not secure information about masturbation, homosexuality or the various pregenital components of the libido, and it is not possible to say, therefore, whether the second kind of hypersexuality bears a fundamental psychological relationship to the first.

In general, the evidence supports the contention that hypersexuality *can* be strongly related to other deviant forms of sexual behavior in women who lack a true heterosexual adequacy. Information as to whether pregenital impulses are stronger in such individuals than in others is unfortunately not available.

THE ANAL CHARACTER

The complexities of Freud's theory of the anal character (1908) need not be reviewed here. The theory is an explanation of what effects on the adult character are caused by the persistence and distortion of the anal component of pregenital libido. Various correlations are predicted by the theory. Among these is one between childhood anal erotism, or constipation, and sadistic-masochistic fantasies or impulses. Another is between the various adult character traits, such as stinginess, orderliness, and stubbornness, that go to make up the so-called anal character. These are supposed to develop by sublimation of, and reaction formation to, the original overstrong anal component.

Hamilton (1929, pp. 467-472) found that 35 of his men and 24 of his women recalled some form of childhood anal erotism, and he has made a rough comparison of the characteristics of these people with those of subjects who could not recall such erotism. Table 4 gives the frequency with which

TABLE 4. Frequency of occurrence of anal traits in persons who could and could not recall childhood anal erotism or constipation. (From Hamilton, 1929, pp. 467–468)

Anal-erotic Trait	Frequency of Occurrence			
	Men		Women	
	Anal (N = 35) %	Nonanal (N = 65) %	Anal (N = 24) %	Nonanal (N = 76) %
Stinginess or extrava- gance	46	37	42	22
Sadism	77	37	54	25
Masochism	74	18	54	21
Fetichism	28	14	33	22
Concern for clothes	87	66	75	70

each of the alleged correlates was present in the anal erotic and nonanal erotic groups. The reference to sadistic and masochistic fantasies, impulses or acts includes both past and present experience; the stinginess or extravagance, which is measured by the subject's report of the spouse's opinion, and both fetichism and concern for clothes relate to adult behavior only. The "clothes" item includes so many conflicting categories that it is of doubtful significance, and the fetichism is not related to anal erotism by theory. It is possible to argue, too, that the correlation with sadism-masochism is a spurious one based on the hypothetical possibility that those who had clearer recall or more recent experiences of the anal erotism might have the same for sadism-masochism. The inadequacy of the trait ratings does not give great confidence in the interpretation of the correlations as dependent on the theoretical relations hypothesized by Freud, but there is no counterevidence, either, and the differences are confirmatory.

In an effort to make a somewhat more accurate test of the predicted correlation between the three cardinal traits of the anal character (stinginess, obstinacy, and orderliness), Sears (1936b)[1] secured ratings of the 37 men in a college fraternity living group. Each man was rated by every other man on a 7-point scale for each of the traits; the average of all the ratings given a man on a trait was taken as the "true" measure of that trait in him. The reliabilities of the ratings were satisfactory as measured by the split-half technique: stinginess $= +.85$, obstinacy $= +.93$, and orderliness $= +.96$. In order to eliminate a generalized halo effect in the ratings a measure of popularity was secured by having each man list the 5 men he liked the most and the 5 he disliked most. By subtracting, for each man, the frequency of the latter nomination from that of the former, it was possible to get a rank order of popularity within the group. When, by use of partial correlation, the halo effect was held constant, the correlations between the three traits were as follows:

Stinginess and orderliness $= +.39$
Stinginess and obstinacy $= +.37$
Obstinacy and orderliness $= +.36$

These correlations are very small but all are positive and in the predicted direction. It is interesting to note, too, that orderliness is considered a desirable trait and the other two are rated as reprehensible by college men. In support of this is the fact that popularity was correlated negatively with stinginess ($-.87$) and obstinacy ($-.56$) but slightly positively with orderliness ($+.20$).

These findings indicate that there is, in a sample of young

[1] Part of these data are previously unpublished.

males, a slight tendency for the anal character traits to form the kind of constellation observed by Freud. Whether the constellation is related to anal erotism is uncertain, but Hamilton's data suggest that it is.

SUBLIMATION

The process by which pregenital impulses such as anal erotic ones are converted into certain of the adult drives is sublimation (Freud, 1905). By this term is meant that the impulses change in such a way as to stimulate "higher," or more socially acceptable, behavior. A subsidiary usage of the term has applied to genital impulses as well.

Little is known about the process itself and but one study has been devoted to its investigation. Taylor (1933) concluded that there should be a correlation between agenitality of behavior and certain of the more refined and intellectual vocations. His reasoning was that sublimation of the more sensuous of the impulses would lead to the socially desirable behavior and that, this being satisfying, the libido would thereby be impoverished as to pregenital or genital impulse. Taylor's reasoning is at some variance with Freud's.

This predicted negative correlation between overt genital activity and intellectual activity (as measured by achievement) did not appear in Taylor's investigation. He secured the cooperation of 40 young unmarried men whose intellectual and characterological achievements were outstanding. They were students, physicians, lawyers and professional men of other kinds. Their intellectual drive was as great as their achievement and, according to Taylor, if ever there was a group which should have renounced genital gratification if sublimation were operative, this was it. The contrary proved to be the case. None of the 40 was completely without sexual gratification, although the majority found their opportunities insufficient. It seems improbable that that would differentiate them from any other group of young unmarried men. Where heterosexual satisfaction was unavailable masturbation was used. In all cases genital sexual behavior was not only common but voluntarily indulged in and sought after.

These results give testimony to the vigor and initiative of young American males, but they bear very little on the Freudian theory of sublimation. No account was taken of pregenital impulses and no comparison was made with men of equal capacity but inferior attainment. The problem of sublimation is still badly in need of investigation.

PARANOIA

Since homosexual impulses are highly disapproved and a person who manifests them ordinarily suffers serious social punishment, such impulses are usually hidden as much as possible. It is presumed that the great majority of people who feel themselves to be somewhat homosexual avoid recognition of the fact themselves. This repression is not always entirely successful, however, and the constant breaking through into consciousness of the forbidden tendency may be accompanied by severe feelings of guilt and anxiety.

Freud (1911) pointed to a not uncommon mechanism by which such anxieties might be eliminated; this was through the medium of denying that the impulses came from the self (projection) and by converting the love emotion into its opposite (reaction-formation). The homosexual reaction was converted from "I love him" to "I hate him," and when this defense proved insufficient, the latter was converted by projection to "He hates me." This final stage of the defensive process is the fullblown paranoia.

As a preliminary to the study of this rather complicated psychological sequence, two investigations have sought to discover whether, in fact, there is any correlation between homosexuality and paranoia. The first, that of Gardner (1931), involved the behavioral examination of 120 hospitalized cases of "paranoid condition" (N = 80) and "paranoid dementia precox" (N = 40). These were consecutive admissions with the exception that no alcoholics with persecutory delusions were included. The frequencies of the overt homosexual behavior and of homosexual symbolism were counted. By the former was meant the occurrence of actual homosexual attacks by the patient, or the delusional statement that others were attacking him in this way. Symbolism was scored as present only when it was "so indicative that probably no psychiatrist would challenge the inference."

The frequencies of the two degrees of homosexuality are indicated in Table 5. A total of 45 per cent were diagnosed

TABLE 5. Incidence of homosexual behavior and symbolism in a paranoid population of both sexes (from Gardner, 1931, p. 60) and in an ordinary psychopathic sample of females. (From Strakosch, 1934, p. 57)

Type of Practice of Homosexuality	Paranoid and Paranoid Precox: Gardner		General Psychopathic: Strakosch
	Male (N = 60) %	Female (N = 60) %	Female (N = 700) %
Positive	51.7	38.7	6.4
Symbolic	30.0	20.0	4.7
Overt	21.7	18.7	1.7
Negative	48.3	61.3	93.6

positive. Gardner gives no control data for the rest of the hospital population, but a rough comparison can be made with the descriptive categories in the study of psychopathic women by Strakosch (1934). In the table, the Strakosch data for married and single women (p. 57, Table 15) are combined. The various degrees and categories of homosexuality are included under "positive"; Strakosch's "non-overt" and "trend" have been subsumed under "symbolism" for tabular convenience although this is probably only a rough approximation to an equating of the two sets of criteria. The "overt" category is the same for both studies.

It will be noted that the paranoids showed far more homosexual behavior than the general psychopathic population which presumably included some paranoids. One must suspect that Strakosch's criteria of homosexuality were more rigid than Gardner's and that his information was more complete.

In order to get a more objective measure of homosexuality, and one that would automatically provide control groups with comparable criteria of measurement, Page and Warkentin (1938) gave the Terman-Miles Masculinity-Femininity test to 50 paranoid men. This test provides a measure of interests and attitudes that differentiate the sexes (Terman and Miles, 1936) and has been given to a number of different groups such as normal adult males, passive homosexuals and active homosexuals. The group of paranoids chosen by Page and Warkentin was matched as nearly as possible to the characteristics of the groups reported by Terman and Miles; the age range was from 20 to 60, mental age was 15-0 or better, and all patients were in good contact with their social environment.

The test scores from this group were pronouncedly feminine, in this respect being more closely associated with those of passive homosexuals than of the normal males or active homosexuals. The best discrimination between the paranoids and Terman and Miles' normals was on Exercise 5, which has also proved most discriminating between passive inverts and normals.

These results confirm those of Gardner. The correlation between paranoid disturbance and homosexuality is established. Whether the mechanism involved is that described by Freud, and whether there are other possible sources of paranoia besides homosexuality, are not revealed by the present data.

An effort was made by Sears (1937a) to extend the relationship between M-F score and paranoid symptoms into the normal range of behavior. He constructed a scale for the measurement of ideas of reference in male college students and, with a group of 50, correlated the scores from it with M-F scores. Although the range on both scales was large, there was no evidence of a relationship. Ideas of reference in the normal person may well be quite unrelated to the persecutory delusions of paranoid psychotics.

CONCLUSIONS

The various quantitative data give support to some and fail to support others of Freud's contentions. On the whole it appears that his clinical observations are confirmed by these wider samplings. Women with inadequate orgasms deviate slightly more from normal sexual practice than do those whose orgasms are adequate, but there is no evidence that they have more anxiety or guilt associated with sex activity. Hypersexual women, selected on a criterion of promiscuity, have definitely more deviant sexual impulses (masturbation, homosexuality) than other women. Paranoid patients have a high record of homosexuality. There is a positive relationship among the traits and pregenital activities dictated by the theory of the anal character.

In spite of the supportive character of the evidence, however, there is much that remains obscure. The truly theoretical aspects of psychoanalysis involve such concepts as inhibition, sublimation, reaction formation and projection. These connecting links between the facts of clinical observation are what make Freud's writings distinctive from those of other students of psychopathology. And yet it is these very concepts that remain hidden in the objective data. Nothing supports them; nothing refutes them.

This may be partly the fault of the data, but fundamentally it is a function of the very nature of the concepts themselves. They represent dynamic relationships between actions and cannot be observed directly. The process of psychoanalysis itself does not give immediate evidence of them but provides infinitely detailed accounts of actions whose interrelations, according to Freud, are *best explained* by such hypothetical processes. The crudeness and meagerness of the available objective data are so great that such concepts do not appear to be the *only possible* explanations. Hence the data do not give the appearance of supporting these aspects of psychoanalytic theory.

It is to the attempts at direct investigation of these dynamic interrelations of actions that the remaining chapters are devoted.

Chapter V

Fixation and Regression

EVEN WHEN sexual development goes through its normal phases and the adult makes an apparently satisfactory heterosexual adjustment, breakdowns sometimes occur. Freud noted that certain of these constitute a return to earlier modes of pleasure-finding, or libidinal gratification. In effect, the patient gives up his adult heterosexuality and returns to an earlier stage of sexual adjustment. This reaction Freud (1920) calls regression.

He was able to specify two of the conditions that were necessary for such an occurrence. The first was *fixation*, i.e., "a particularly close attachment of the instinct to its object" (Freud, 1915a). The second was *frustration*, i.e., the prevention of satisfaction for the instinct. If a man had had a strong attachment to his mother but then made the customary shift to a wife, he might regress to the earlier object (mother) if he were frustrated in his efforts to gain gratification from the later one (wife). This may be called *object regression*.

Freud (1920) distinguished a second kind of regression, however, that involved not only a change of object but a change of the erotogenic zone that served as the source of stimulation. He spoke of this as a "return of the entire sexual organization to an earlier stage of development." In this case a person who had reached the stage of genital sexuality might regress to the anal stage, relinquishing not only the genital libidinal objects but the genital zone as a source of gratification. This may be called *drive regression*.

Still a third kind of regression can be described, although Freud did not include it in his discussion. Its discovery came directly from the efforts of experimental psychologists to subject the general notion of regression to more rigorous investigation; it has been called, variously, retrogression (Barker, Dembo and Lewin, 1941), habit regression (Mowrer, 1940) and instrumental act regression (Sears, 1941). The latter term simply indicates the aspect of the behavior sequence that is involved in the regression. Any sequence includes 1) the original instigation or drive, 2) the goal response, 3) the object necessary for the performance of the goal response, and 4) the instrumental acts that put the organism into appropriate context with the goal object so the goal response may be performed. If the drive and object both remain the same following frustration, it is still possible for the instrumental acts to revert to a previous form. For example, a five-year-old may resume his crawling to wrest parental attention from a younger sib, or an author accustomed to a typewriter may revert to longhand on a difficult piece of writing. From an experimental standpoint, these changes are analogous to a white rat's return to a previously relinquished path through a maze. This third type of regression will be called *instrumental act regression* here in order to keep clearly in mind the particular aspect of the behavior sequence that is changed following frustration.

The amount of research on these three kinds of regression has been very unequal for various reasons. Nothing has been done with drive regression or fixation; sex development cannot be modified for experimental purposes in children, and its pattern in the lower animals is too different from that of man to permit cross reference. Object fixation has been touched on, but scarcely more. Instrumental act fixation and regression, however, have both been studied intensively, perhaps because the techniques for the control and study of *movement* and *learning* are far more advanced than those for the control and study of *drive*.

OBJECT FIXATION

The significance of fixation, if by that is meant a superlatively strong habit, lies in its role as an obstacle to social growth and as an important antecedent to regression. An attachment to the mother, for example, can be important either because it prevents the development of normal sexual adjustments with contemporaries or because interference with an established adult adjustment will more likely be followed by a return to the earlier attachment—possibly with a reactivation of the anxieties that were necessarily associated with its overcoming. But a fixation must be considered a relative matter, not an absolute one. Object attachments or instrumental acts have some *degree of strength;* they are not to be thought of as involving either fixation or no fixation.

1. *Development of object fixations.* Experimental work with animals has cast more light on the origins of object attachments than on the conditions of their strength. As Freud (1905) pointed out in connection with the development of infantile object cathexes, those persons or objects that are associated with gratification become loved for themselves alone. This is a process of acquiring secondary reward value.

A number of examples of this process have been reported by students of animal learning. K. A. Williams (1929) taught rats to "like" a white box by always feeding them in the white side of a black and white discrimination apparatus. The evidence that the white box had itself taken on reward qualities was secured by demonstrating that the rats would learn a maze in order to reach it. After having been practiced for several days on the discrimination apparatus the rats were put into an unpainted redwood maze. They were never rewarded in the maze and apparently learned nothing. When, on the ninth day, the white box was put at the end of the maze, however, the rats immediately ran to it. The quickness with which they then learned the maze indicated there had been some latent learning, and the fact that they learned so much more rapidly than they had been learning (without the white box), indicated that the box had reward value. Eventually, since the rats were never fed in the white box after running through the maze, the box lost its value and the number of errors made in running the maze increased again.

2. *Strength of fixation.* A somewhat different demonstration of the same general principle was made by Wolfe (1936) in the course of discovering one of the factors that determines the strength of the attachment to objects. He trained chimpanzees to drop poker chips into a slot in a vending machine in order to secure grapes. The fact that these poker chips really developed reward value and were "desired" by the animals was evidenced in two ways: 1) the animals would *work* to get the chips, and 2) the chips could be used as a reward to make the animals *learn* a new task. (Cf. Cowles, 1937.)

Wolfe was able to increase the strength of attachment to, or desire for, the chips by increasing the amount of primary food reward used in the associative training. By doubling the number of grapes given for a chip of one color, the animals were evidently taught to like those chips better than those of another color for which only a single grape was secured. The evidence for this conclusion was that, in a free choice situation, the animals would choose the double-value chips rather than the single-value ones. The general principle exemplified by this experiment is that the strength of attachment to an object, i.e., its secondary reward value, varies positively with the amount of primary reward with which it is associated.

3. *Interference effect of object fixations.* Although the problem of interference between habits has received intensive study with reference to both remembering and motor learning, there is little information about its effects in connection with object attachments. It has been demonstrated, however, that attachment to one object may interfere with the development of an attachment to another. This is particularly true with reference to foods.

Again it is from animal psychology that critical data come. Elliott (1928) trained 2 groups of white rats to run through a 14-unit multiple-T maze for a food reward. Group A was given bran mash and Group B sunflower seeds. The two different foods appeared to be equally satisfactory for the two groups learned with approximately equal rapidity during the first ten days. On the tenth day, however, Group A was shifted to sunflower seeds. At once its error and time scores began to increase. The original sunflower group continued to improve. On the seventeenth day Group A was returned to its bran mash reward and within three days it had regained its former equality with Group B. It is especially noteworthy than when Group A was shifted unexpectedly to sunflower seeds it not only became worse immediately but *during the following days it became still worse.* The breakdown of the maze habit was progressive when the rats were being forced to accept a new object.

It should not be supposed that this situation is common to all learning experiments in which one habit is replaced by another. One habit can give way to another and objects are often relinquished in real life. Elliott's data do point up an extremely important problem, however: what are the conditions that determine whether there will be interference with or facilitation of the development of new object attachments? When does affection for the cross-sex parent facilitate and when does it interfere with heterosexual adjustment? (Cf. Chapter III, p. 1.) The answers to this question will be complex in the extreme and probably can come only from intensive work by students of animal learning and motivation.

INSTRUMENTAL ACT FIXATION

The problem of habit strength has engrossed the attention of animal psychologists because of its obvious pertinence tô the prediction and control of learned behavior and, in its human application, the educative process. As habit strength is customarily measured, it is equivalent to strength of instrumental act, and this latter is the quantitative continuum at one end of which lies what Freud called fixation, i.e., great strength.

The chief measure of instrumental act strength is *degree of resistance to change* either by extinction (nonreward) or by retraining (reward of an incompatible habit). This is essentially the criterion of fixation used in the clinical situation; a child is said to have a mother-fixation if he is resistant either to changing to another person or to relinquishing the mother. This "resistance" refers to resistance in the face of normally reasonable amounts of social pressure, persuasion and reward. Obviously these influences are not easily measured but the clinician accustomed to observing such behavior makes rough judgments of normality on a statistical basis.

A number of different factors have been shown to influence the strength of instrumental acts in white rats and these can be listed without undue complication. Presumably they would be of importance in determining the strength of human instrumental acts as well.

1. *Amount of reinforcement.* Chronologically, the first

variable to be related specifically to fixation was the amount of reinforcement given to a habit. Krechevsky and Honzik (1932) constructed a simple choice box, for rats, shaped like a reversed letter F. The two alleys turning off the main stem were interchangeable. Three groups of rats were trained to take the shorter of the two alleys to get food, and then the positions of the alleys were interchanged and the rats were forced to learn to go to the position they had previously avoided. The three groups were given different amounts of training on the first habit and it was found that the difficulty of changing their behavior was directly related to the amount of training they had had.

In this experimental situation the original instrumental act was running down the stem of the choice box and turning into the short alley. The rat was motivated by hunger and this behavior put him in context with the goal object (food) so that he could perform the goal response (eating). Each time it occurred, this goal response served to reinforce the instrumental acts immediately preceding it; the greater the number of trials, the greater the reinforcement. The fact that those animals that had most trials on the original reaction were most difficult to retrain is taken to mean that the greater the amount of reinforcement, the greater is the strength of the instrumental acts.

The same principle was demonstrated by Youtz (1938) and S. B. Williams (1938) with a different technique. They used a box in which a rat could get food pellets out of a kind of vending machine simply by pressing down a bar that jutted out from the wall. Once he was in the box, the rat could get as many pellets as he wanted and at whatever rate he wanted. Pressing the bar was the instrumental act.

Youtz permitted one group of rats to practice the habit 10 times and another group 40 times. He then arranged the apparatus so that no more food would come down the chute when the bar was pressed, and counted the number of times the rats in the two groups pressed the bar before giving up. This was a measure of the strength of the habit in terms of its resistance to experimental extinction. Youtz found, as did Williams in a later and more elaborate study, that the rats with more training were more resistant to the extinction process.

These experiments are far removed from the vividness and color of human behavior. The dogged perseverance of the aspiring novelist, the exasperating tenacity of a child in a temper tantrum, the pathetic confusion of the old workman faced with new tools seem almost unrelated to these mechanical rodents. But the difference is apparent only, and it is important to examine the various other factors that determine the strength of instrumental acts.

2. *Strength of drive at time of learning.* Some evidence has been obtained by Finan (1940) that instrumental acts are more strongly established by a given number of reinforcements when the drive is strong than when it is weak. Four groups of rats were deprived of food for 1, 12, 24 and 48 hours, respectively. At the end of this deprivation period they were allowed to learn the bar-pressing technique described above. All groups were given 30 reinforcements and then, after 24 hours, all were extinguished by being allowed to press the bar without getting any food. The 1 hour group was least resistant to extinction and the 12 hour group was the most. The 24 and 48 hour groups were approximately equal but were a little less resistant than the 12 hour group; i.e., the relation was somewhat curvilinear. Roughly, however, the stronger the drive was at the time of learning, the stronger was the habit.

3. *Amount of reward.* One of the factors that determines

the amount of physical work an animal will do is the amount of reward given. Fletcher (1940) found that chimpanzees were quite sensitive to relatively small differences and Cowles and Nissen (1937) found that the accuracy of a delayed response can vary with size of reward. No evidence has yet been presented that the strength of a habit varies with this factor but it is not an unreasonable supposition.

4. *Interval between instrumental act and goal response.* Another aspect of the learning situation is the interval between the performance of the instrumental act and the appearance of the reward that permits occurrence of the goal response. Skinner (1936) has shown that when a delay is introduced between the rat's act of pressing down the bar and the actual delivery of the food pellet, there is a reduction in the act's later resistance to extinction. The amount of weakening was found to be roughly proportional to the length of delay. These results are consistent with other findings that discrimination habits are harder to develop and maintain when rewards are delayed.

5. *Frequency of reinforcement.* Each time a goal response occurs there is reinforcement of the instrumental acts preceding it. The problem of specifying just what composes the instrumental acts is difficult, however; in effect all activity preceding the goal response appears to come under this heading and to undergo reinforcement. If a given *movement* must be performed twice before the goal is reached, then the *pair* of movements becomes the instrumental act to the goal response. If, later, these acts are repeatedly performed without any reward occurring, it is to be expected that more *single* movements would occur during the extinction process if a *pair* of movements was the unit that had originally been reinforced than if a *single* movement had been the unit. Evidence to support this view had been obtained by Humphreys

(1939a, 1939b) in experiments with the conditioned eyelid reflex and with expectancy judgments.

6. *Punishment.* When punishment immediately follows an act, that act is normally supposed to undergo a certain weakening; but when punishment occurs during the progress of the act, there is evidence that behavior becomes more stereotyped. Hamilton and Krechevsky (1933) found that when rats were learning to go to the opposite branch of a single-unit T-maze from the branch they had originally preferred, they became very fixed in their choices if shock were regularly administered just before the choice-point. The direction of the stereotyped behavior was not consistently either toward or away from the shorter of two alleys nor was it consistently in the direction of the previous training. It was simply fixed, rigidified; the rats repeated what they did when they were shocked. Everall (1935) used as punishment a delay period at the choice-point in a single-unit T-maze. Food reward was available on both sides of the T. A control group was not delayed. On test, the experimental group showed greater consistency in choice of direction to turn, i.e., they were more stereotyped. Fairlie (1937) trained rats to make a black-white discrimination and then shocked them at the moment of choice. Half were shocked when they made correct responses and the other half when they made incorrect ones. Learning in both groups was retarded, and the rats returned to highly consistent position habits, more in the shock-right group than in the shock-wrong.

Whether the delay in Everall's study can be considered as punishment in the same psychological sense as electric shock is an open question. The effects are comparable, and they support the generalization that when punishment of a disruptive kind occurs, behavior becomes rigidified. It is possible that

some clinical fixations are simply the responses that inter-
vened as a consequence of punishment.

7. *Sub-goal reinforcement.* As was described in connection
with object fixation, an object that repeatedly accompanies
a reward takes on the properties of a goal-object itself. In
such case it is described as a sub-goal. Since it possesses re-
inforcing power in its own right, it is reasonable to suppose
that there would be greater resistance to extinction if the sub-
goal were present during the extinction test. Bugelski (1938)
has shown that such is the case. Two groups of rats were
paired on the basis of their speed of learning the bar-pressing
technique for obtaining food pellets. During the training
series a "click" accompanied each pellet's fall into the trough.
One group was extinguished with the "click" still occurring
after each depression of the bar and the other group was
extinguished with the sound absent. The former group was
much more resistant to extinction. Hence, it may be said that
instrumental acts are stronger if sub-goals as well as primary
ones are reached than if there are no sub-goal reinforcements.

8. *Hierarchical position of habits.* When a defense (avoidance) reaction is formed with the aid of primary motivation,
e.g., escape from shock, it is possible to transfer the response
to many other stimuli besides the ones to which the primary
conditioning occurs (Finch and Culler, 1934). This can be
achieved by presenting the conditioned or signal stimulus
and a second neutral stimulus at the same time. The response
that had been learned to the first stimulus is now transferred
to the second as well. This procedure permits the development of a hierarchy of stimuli (first, second, third order, etc.)
if some extra energizing stimulus is presented when the animal fails to respond appropriately. In a study by Brogden
and Culler (1935) dogs were trained to lift a foreleg to a
neutral stimulus by shocking the paw. This action became

a response to three other stimuli in turn by simple association plus a shock on the thorax when the response failed to occur. The primary defense reaction proved to be considerably stronger than the secondary, tertiary or quaternary reactions, which were all approximately equal in resistance. Brogden (1939) repeated the experiment, using food as the energizing stimulus, i.e., reward instead of punishment, and found that the various responses differed in resistance in the order of formation, the primary being strongest and the quaternary weakest. In general, it seems probable that the more primitive an instrumental act is, i.e., the nearer to a primary position in the hierarchy of learning, the stronger it will prove to be.

9. *Generalization.* A slight transfer effect in the learning of two similar instrumental acts has been demonstrated by S. B. Williams (1941b); this serves to strengthen the habits reciprocally. He found that a relatively weak habit of pressing a horizontal bar to get food gained some strength from the learning of a similar habit, that of pressing a vertical bar; this held true whether the habit that was measured was learned first or second, or whether it was the horizontal or the vertical bar. The transfer effects either disappeared or became negative when the initial strength of the tested habit was high, and therefore this factor of generalization may have little importance for the problem of fixation.

10. *Interval between learning and extinction.* Youtz (1938) found that rats trained in the bar-pressing act were more resistant to extinction when the extinction trials were given 15 days after the learning than when they were given 1 day after. This was true with groups that had been given either 10 or 40 reinforcements in the original learning. Brogden (1940) has obtained similar results. It is doubtful, however, whether these findings can be translated to mean that early habits, never subjected either to further reinforcement or to

extinction, will be more strongly fixated than later learned habits, since these experimental findings have to do with relatively brief intervals. It is more likely that the rat behavior can be explained in terms of the effects of massed and distributed practice than of true habit age.

11. *Effect of previous extinctions.* Although it is possible to eliminate an instrumental act by preventing the occurrence of the goal response, a period of elapsed time following the extinction will permit a spontaneous recovery of the act. Youtz (1938) and S. B. Williams (1938) have shown that these spontaneously recovered habits are much weaker than the original not-previously-extinguished habit. Youtz gave a second extinction series 24 hours after the first, and a third one 55 days after the second. There was progressively less resistance to extinction. Williams gave a second extinction series an hour after the first with similar results.

Ellson (1938) and Youtz (1939) have shown that the process of generalization operates with reference to extinction as well as to reinforcement. The method of both investigators was the same: two brass bars, vertical and horizontal, were built into a rat box and the animals were trained to operate both of them. A fully trained rat could get food, therefore, by pressing either bar. One bar was then removed from the box and the response to the remaining bar was extinguished. The removed bar was replaced and the response to it was extinguished. Under such conditions the second bar response was much less resistant than the first. S. B. Williams (1941a) has found, however, that the amount of influence from the earlier extinction is in part a function of the original strength of the habits.

It appears, then, that a previous extinction of any instrumental act weakens the response and, further, that previous extinctions of similar responses in the same stimulus situation have virtually the same effect.

12. *Strength of drive at time of extinction.* In an attempt to determine whether a stronger drive at the time of extinction would increase resistance to extinction, Sackett (1939) trained two groups of rats on the bar-pressing habit under exactly similar conditions. One group was then extinguished 6 hours after a meal and the other group 30 hours after. The latter was somewhat more resistant but the data showed unusual variability. G. L. Heathers and Arakelian (1941) have verified the principle with a similar technique, however. In addition they were able to demonstrate some slight differential effect on strength of habit produced by partial extinction at different drive strengths. One group of rats was given a series of extinction trials under strong drive conditions and another group, similarly trained, was given the same number under weak drive. When the two groups were finally tested for resistance to extinction, the latter was more resistant.

It appears, then, that a habit is stronger when the drive is strong but that any extinction occurring under strong drive is more effective than under weak drive, i.e., a habit is more severely weakened by partial extinction under the former conditions than under the latter.

INSTRUMENTAL ACT REGRESSION

The cogency of Freud's statement about the relation of fixation and regression now becomes clear. When an animal is faced with an obstacle to further action, i.e., when it is frustrated, it must necessarily perform a new instrumental act. This new act may be either a previously discarded one or a completely novel assembly of habit segments. In any case, whatever may be the chronological origin of the behavior, the act that occurs will be the one that has the largest net residue of "strength" from the dozen factors described above as determiners of instrumental act fixation. But if the act is one that had previously been discarded and is therefore *older* than the frustrated act, instrumental act regression is said to have occurred. Since only relatively strong instrumental acts can intervene in this way, regression may be said to depend on previous fixation.

1. *Shock frustration.* The first demonstration and theoretical discussion of this process was that of Hamilton and Krechevsky (1933). They trained rats to choose the shorter of two alleys in a single-unit T-maze and then reversed the sides. A control group simply learned the new position while an experimental group was always shocked at the choice point after the new learning had definitely started. In this latter group more than half the animals suddenly reverted to the former direction of turning although it now led them through the longer alley to the food reward. The authors interpreted this as a form of regression to a previously learned habit but suggested it might be reversion to original position habits. A second experimental group, treated somewhat differently from the first, gave support to the latter interpretation.

In order to determine more definitely whether the hypothesized position habits were more important than previous learning in directionalizing the postshock (frustration) behavior, Sanders (1937) trained 5 rats, by a differential delay method, to turn in the direction of their original position habits on a T-choice apparatus. After learning was complete the direction of turning was reversed, and when this new learning was well started the animals were shocked at the choice point. Four of the animals regressed at once and the fifth one regressed when shock was withdrawn. The animals were then given enough training on the second habit so that practice on the two directions of turning was equivalent. Shock presented during a series of trials congruent with the original position habits did not produce regression to the *learned* habit.

Sanders suggested that regression is limited to genetically primary habits, but the data seem not to warrant so drastic a conclusion. The shock did not actually prevent the continuation of the ongoing activity in either case and therefore the occurrence of regression would depend on whether the punishment was adequate to reduce the effective strength of the ongoing response below that of the alternative. Since both habits had had equal practice, any difference in strength would have to be a function of some initial innate difference. The initial position habits would account for the extra strength of the so-called *genetically primary* response. The shock was evidently of sufficient inhibiting value to reduce the momentarily greater strength of the purely learned habit and thus permit the prepotency of the position habit to effect a regression. The shock was not strong enough, however, to reverse this effect.

Sanders tested also for the effects of *generalization* of the effect of shock by shocking the animals in another box and then putting them in the discrimination unit to test for regression. There was no evidence of regression. Mowrer (1940) has suggested that the shock was not a sufficient frustration to produce regression except when it was presented during the actual response sequence where it could interfere with the important anticipatory or expectancy reactions.

Mowrer's own demonstration of regression relied on shock as the frustrating agent but it served to produce frustration not simply by being painful but by interfering with well-established escape-from-other-shock behavior. One group of 5 rats was permitted to learn by trial-and-error that the electric shock in the grill on which they stood could be turned off by pressing a foot pedal that was hinged to the cage wall. Another group was given shocks for an approximately equal amount of time but had no pedal to press. These latter rats learned to sit up on their hind legs to escape the shock. When this defensive technique had been well learned they were permitted to learn how to use the foot pedal. Then both groups were frustrated by having shock introduced to this foot pedal, so that when they tried to turn off the floor shock they got a shock from the instrument of salvation. The rats that had originally learned to escape by standing on their hind legs almost immediately regressed to that habit while the other rats continued to press the pedal. A third group of rats that suffered shock on the pedal from the very beginning of their training at escape from floor shock "voted" 4 out of 5 to use the pedal rather than the hind leg standing as a method of avoiding punishment. These results seem to indicate that regression can occur to a previously learned response that is not "genetically primary" as measured by a preponderance of free choices.

Final evidence that regression is a function of strength comes from a recent investigation by Martin (1940, Experiment II). Three groups of 5 rats were trained in a T-unit to make a choice congruent with their original position habits. They were then reversed, trained to make the opposite response. The 3 groups were differentiated by the relative amount of training given on the two habits; the ratio of the strengths varied. When shock was administered at the choice point during the operation of the second habit, regression occurred to some degree in all 3 groups, but the number of rats that regressed was a function of the relative strength of the first habit. In an even more spectacular test, Martin (1940, Experiment I) found that only 2 rats in 30 regressed to a "native hypothesis" after the opposite hypothesis had been over-trained and then shock administered as a frustration. Further, after this stereotyping shock, it was more difficult to train the rats to use a third and irrelevant hypothesis than it had been to train them to use the second one, even though the second had been in direct opposition to the "native" one, i.e., the rat's own spontaneous selection.

A careful analysis of different methods of controlling the relative strengths of the habits and of inducing frustration has been made by O'Kelly (1940a, 1940b). He used a circular field 7 feet in diameter into which a rat was introduced from the side. It could then cross to a reward box at either side of the circle and get food or water, depending on which drive was being used. The rat was trained to go first to one side and then retrained to go to the other. The same strength of hunger drive was used in both cases. Shock was administered during the performance of the second habit, and almost half the subsequent trials (10/24) were regressive. In view of the findings of Martin the absolute frequency becomes unimportant, but O'Kelly found that the regressive responses were much faster and more direct across the open field than were the "perseverative" responses, i.e., the repetition of the second habit. With subsquent groups O'Kelly used the thirst drive and varied the strength of motivation under which the first or second habit, or both, were learned. Although learning was always carried to the same criterion, strength of the response, as measured by presence or absence of regression following shock in the second habit, appeared to be definitely a function of the strength of drive under which learning occurred. This supports the results of Finan's (1940) study cited above in connection with fixation.

2. *Removal of reward.* The above experiments have relied on electric shock as the frustrating agent, but removal of

reward can be equally efficacious. Hull (1934) trained rats to run along a straight 40 foot alley to get food. The speed of running through consecutive 5 foot sections was measured and it was found that a clear speed gradient existed during the early trials; the rats started slowly but speeded up as they neared the goal and then slowed again just at the end. This gradient virtually disappeared after several days of practice, but reappeared almost at once when the food was removed from the goal and the animals were no longer rewarded.

Another group of rats was trained in the same way but the alley was only 20 feet long. Removal of reward produced the same effects. These rats were then trained on the full 40 foot alley. At first there was a considerable slowing up at the 20 foot point where the gradient had ended before, but this soon disappeared and the time scores for consecutive sections of the alley were very like those of the other group after lengthy training, i.e., the gradient in speed-of-locomotion had disappeared. When these rats were frustrated, however, they regressed to the "hump" pattern of the gradient; they were evidently regressing to the behavior learned in the original series of trials on the 20 foot alley. Miller and Miles (1936), using a maze, obtained somewhat similar consequences from removal of reward and also from alcohol.

3. *Satiation.* Even satiation can serve as a method of reducing the strength of a response and thus permit the occurrence of a previously relinquished response. O'Kelly (1940b) trained a group of 8 rats to run in one direction and when that habit was well learned he reversed the direction. When this new habit had been learned the rats were satiated and tested again. All 8 rats regressed to the previously learned response. On the following day, with the customary motivation, they again performed the second habit.

4. *Interpretation.* These various demonstrations of the

reactivation of previously learned and then discarded habit patterns suggest that the problem of *instrumental act regression* is primarily one of *instrumental act strength*. Frustration is significant only in so far as it serves, *first,* to give rise to a situation in which a change of response is necessary or possible, and *second,* to reduce the strength of actions that have immediately preceded it. Both of the methods of frustration illustrated by these studies, electric shock and removal of reward, presumably interfere with the expectancy of reward; shock does this by direct interference with anticipatory goal responses in progress, and removal of reward does it by gradual extinction of the anticipations. In both cases the effect of reducing the reward expectancy is to reduce the strength of instigation to the instrumental act, leaving other acts prepotent.

Shock and removal of reward differ in one way, however, in their effects on strength of habit. Since shock disrupts and hence eliminates the reward expectancies (anticipatory goal responses), the total effective strength of instigation to the ongoing response is reduced somewhat and the external instigators present immediately following the shock are left solely responsible for determining which instrumental act is to occur. Whichever one does occur *may* be reinforced because it represented, temporally, an *escape* from shock (possibly a reduction of anxiety). Removal of reward, on the other hand, only eliminates the anticipatory goal responses by extinction, but fails to reinforce the response to external instigators as well. Removal of reward thus has greater *eventual* influence than pre-choice shock in reducing strength of response. These facts suggest that, while pre-choice shock gives the appearance of strengthening the response, or of producing strong regression, in effect it has simply created a momentary discrepancy between two competing responses;

removal of reward, on the other hand, gives a straightforward picture of permanently reducing the effective strength of the habit.

From the standpoint of frustration, neither shock nor removal of reward forces an animal to relinquish an act but the experimental conditions always permit it. So long as the frustrations involved do not actually compel a change, their only influence can be in reduction of strength of the ongoing instrumental act. If a frustration should be an actual blockage, however, the problem with respect to regression would still be one of strength of fixation, but then it would be a question as to whether the next act that occurred would be an old and previously discarded one (regression) or a new assembly of habit segments.

It is apparent, then, that regression is a purely descriptive term. It alone does not indicate the dynamics lying beneath the phenomena it describes. These dynamics relate, as has been shown, to the complex interaction of various sources of instigation and inhibition; fundamentally they are the dynamics of the learning process. The data and logic support strongly Freud's statement that regression is a function of fixation—habit strength—but it is a function of frustration in a secondary way only, and what effect frustration has is primarily in the direction of influencing the strength of instrumental act sequences.

PRIMITIVATION

In his use of the term regression, Freud appears to have included two quite different phenomena without making a systematic distinction between them. One is the *reactivation of specific habits,* as discussed above, and the other is a *primitivation of action.* Both represent a change toward less complexity of behavior, but the mechanisms responsible for the change are at least superficially different. Under frustrating conditions, according to Barker, Dembo and Lewin (1941), behavior becomes relatively disorganized, vague rather than specific, scanty in detail, restricted as to area of activities and interest, and decreasingly realistic. These changes are often roughly the same as a return to earlier behavior patterns because the behavior of infancy and early childhood can be described by the same adjectives. Thus if an adult is severely frustrated and returns to the interests and activities of his youth he undergoes a primitivation of action. The significant aspect of the regression phenomenon is not the reactivation of earlier learned actions but the primitivation; in fact, because the adult is never able to behave exactly as a child for reasons of size and language skills, Barker, Dembo and Lewin consider that all regressive behavior merely *simulates* earlier actions. (Cf. Wells, 1935.)

Barker, Dembo and Lewin have given a demonstration of these behavioral changes by frustrating children's playing with toys. As a child becomes older his play becomes more organized, contains more elaborate phantasies, and involves larger and more differentiated units of action. These changes are fairly continuous with increasing age and were used in making a scale for measuring constructiveness (maturity) of play with a standard set of toys. The units of scoring were months and therefore a child's play could be scored on a "play age" scale analogous to mental age.

For the investigation of regression thirty preschool children were frustrated in a free-play situation. The experiment was performed on two successive days. On the first the child was brought into the large experimental room and allowed to play alone with some toys, without assistance or interference, for a half hour. He was then returned to his schoolroom. On the following day he was brought to the room again, but this time one end of the room had been rearranged in such a way as to give a new place to play and in this new place was a set of wonderfully desirable toys, far finer than the ones of the day before. The child was allowed to play with these for 15 minutes, and then, without warning or explanation, the experimenter led the child back to his original play space at the other end of the room and left him there to play with the original much less attractive toys for a half hour. All this time the fine toys were visible through a coarse wire screen that had been lowered across the end of the room between them and the child.

This situation was frustrating, of course, and the final half hour of play with the original toys, which were the standard toys of the play constructiveness scale, permitted a measure of the maturity level. The play during the first day was used as a control. There was considerable difference between the constructiveness of the two days, the average decrement being 17.3 months. Since the children varied from 28 to 61 months in chronological age, this represents a relatively severe regression. The younger children showed less reduction in constructiveness than the older, of course.

It seems probable that this type of regression can eventually be explained by learning principles, and that it should not be considered altogether separately from the reactivation of specific habits. For the present, however, learning theory is not sufficiently advanced for this task, and research performed without reference to such interpretation can aid in isolating variables to be incorporated at a later time in a systematic account of regressive behavior.

HYPNOTIC AGE REGRESSION

An altogether different approach to age regression has been exemplified in a study by Platonow (1933). In this case a much greater primitivation was sought; adults were required to regress to childhood. The primitivation was created by hypnotic suggestion, however, rather than by direct frustration, and was measured with reference to intelligence rather than play constructiveness.

Platonow hynotized three adults and told them they were three years old. In order to determine whether such suggestions had truly led to regression, the subjects were given standard intelligence tests. The scores were close to three years mental age. P. C. Young (1940), skeptical of Platonow's interpretation that this apparent reduction in test score represented a regression of the total personality, repeated the experiment under more carefully controlled conditions. He found that his own subjects were considerably less accurate in their regression on a Stanford-Binet intelligence test than Platonow's subjects had been. Young's 9 college freshmen, instructed under hypnosis to be 3 years old, gave an average mental age of 5 years, 11 months. The range was from 4-7 to 6-9. As a control, Young instructed 7 unhypnotized subjects to simulate such a performance. Their average mental age was 5 years, 5 months, the range being from 4-5 to 6-9. The two groups were handled in the same way except for the hypnosis.

Whether it is possible by suggestion to reactivate the total behavior pattern, i.e., to reinstate the personality, of an adult's 3-year-old self is a moot question. It seems improbable because of the extensive overlaying of earlier reaction patterns by later ones that are similar but just different enough to interfere with the retention and recall of the original ones. No measure of skill, no matter how objective it may be, will be of critical significance as a test of such regression if the childish form of the skill is merely less efficient than that of the adult. Lack of efficiency on a particular task can be achieved in the absence of any total regression; it can occur voluntarily or through lack of motivation. To be of any importance as a research instrument, hypnotic regression must be demonstrated to provide a reactivation of childhood behavior for which the skill or performance ability has lapsed during the growing-up process.

SCHIZOPHRENIA

Still another source of data for age regression exists, at least according to theory. Among the mental disorders, the schizophrenias have been supposed by Fenichel (1934, pp. 316-319) to represent a regression of the total personality to the period before the ego was completely formed. This is a psychopathological analogy to the alleged hypnotic regression. The regression of schizophrenia is one of affect, however, and no adequate objective measures of adult and child affect have been devised.

In an effort to secure some critical measure of schizophrenic behavior that could be compared with that of children, Cameron (1938a, 1938b) investigated some simple forms of thinking. He presented a number of incompleted sentences to patients who had been diagnosed schizophrenic and compared the logical nature of the completions with that of children's. Piaget has shown that there are three ways in which "because" sentences can be completed:

a. *Cause and effect* explanation. "A man fell down in the road because he stumbled."

b. *Logical justification* by appeal from one principle to another. "That animal is not dead because it is moving."

c. *Psychological motivation.* "A boy threw a stone at me because he wanted to hit me."

These three methods of explanation differ in the frequency of their occurrence in children. From Table 6 it will be seen

TABLE 6. Frequency, in per cent, of three types of explanation in normal children and in schizophrenics. (From Cameron, 1938a)

Type of explanation	Children	Schizophrenics
Cause and effect	7.5	45
Logical justification	9.0	23
Motivation	83.5	32

that cause and effect is relatively uncommon in comparison with motivation, which is by far the commonest with children. It is apparent that the reasoning of the schizophrenics, as a group, differed greatly from that of the children.

In order to get a more detailed analysis of the relationship, Cameron divided his patients into three groups according to severity of their disorder. There was no consistent difference, however, except that cause and effect was somewhat more frequent in the "severe" group and logical justification was less so. There were no differences in the frequency of motivational explanations.

Still another comparison was made, this time by presenting incomplete sentences that were designed to suggest a particular form of explanation, either cause and effect or motivation. The schizophrenics proved to have more difficulty in completing the latter than the former, in comparison with the 7 to 9 year old children tested by Piaget, and Cameron concluded that there was a greater disturbance of the childish than of the adult process of explanation. From Cameron's report it is difficult to tell how much similarity there was between his and Piaget's sentences, however, and these differences in frequency may in part depend on differences in degree of objective-subjective relationship between the two experimental materials.

Cameron made various other comparisons, not radically different from these, but in each case the schizophrenics' explanations seemed more nearly to approximate those of the adult than those of the child. This represents a study of only one aspect of the thinking process, the *explanation,* and such matters as symbolism and concept formation have yet to be examined. For the present, however, it must be said that schizophrenic thinking is not a simple regression to childish forms.

One other effort has been made to relate schizophrenia to regression, that of DuBois and Forbes (1934). They studied the postures of catatonic patients during sleep on the hypothesis that there might be a regression to the foetal position. Whatever may have been the origin of this curious theory, the investigators found that only 9 per cent of the total number of postures and 6 per cent of the total sleeping time represented foetal position. This did not differ materially from the frequency observed in the single normal man available as a control.

There is little reason, on the basis of these various data, to attempt to reach a conclusion concerning the relation of schizophrenia to regression. The psychoanalytic theory is related primarily to affect, not posture or thinking, and little can be said of its validity until more relevant investigations have been made.

CONCLUSIONS

The success with which animal psychologists have attacked fixation and regression is dimmed somewhat by the fact that experimental regression is not entirely representative of the Freudian clinical phenomenon. There is sufficient systematic relation between them, however, to suggest that most of the experimental findings can be applied safely to the latter.

If fixation is defined as an unusually strong object attachment, or instrumental act, regression can be considered as the reactivation of a fixated but previously relinquished response following the weakening of a later established response. The weakening, as has been shown, can be secured through frustration by punishment, frustration by removal of reward, satiation or alcohol. When the ongoing response is weakened by any of these four factors, other responses become prepotent; and if the ensuing response is one that was strong at some earlier date, the change in behavior is called regression. These experimental findings give sound support to Freud's contention that regression is a function of fixation, and they suggest that his notion of the importance of frustration is correct as far as it goes but is not the only factor that can give opportunity for fixation to play its role.

The experimental literature contains excellent demonstrations of the way in which *object fixation* to neutral objects develops. One variable, at least, has been shown to be important in determining its strength: the amount of primary reward with which the previously neutral object is associated and for which it becomes a symbol.

An examination of the data relating to a number of variables that influence *instrumental act strength,* suggests that the following factors can be considered significant for the clinical phenomenon of fixation:

1. Amount of reinforcement
2. Strength of drive at time of learning
3. Interval between instrumental act and goal response
4. Punishment during the instrumental act
5. Sub-goal reinforcement
6. Hierarchical position of the act
7. Generalization of reinforcement
8. Generalization of extinction
9. Strength of drive at time of extinction

These facts supplement rather than verify Freud's formulation of the fixation problem.

Experiments based on an alternative conception of regression, that of *primitivation,* demonstrate an important type of human regression, and have considerable significance for the understanding of frustration reactions in general. Efforts to study such phenomena by means of "hypnotic age regression" appear fruitless, however.

Schizophrenia, as a disorder of regression, remains to be studied from the standpoint of affect. Neither the thought processes nor sleeping postures indicate a regressive process, but these are not the most appropriate levels of behavior for testing the theory.

Chapter VI

Repression

WHEN A PARENT punishes a child severely for some forbidden act, the impulse that led to the act in the first place becomes, by association, a stimulus for anxiety reactions. Since any anxiety is painful, trial-and-error behavior may be initiated with the aim of eliminating the discomfort. The number of possible solutions to this difficulty are limited, however, because the actual source of the anxiety is an impulse within the person himself. Freud described three main techniques that are used: 1) flight from any external stimuli that aid in arousing the impulse, 2) voluntary rejection of the impulse, and 3) involuntary *repression* of both the impulse itself and all consciousness of its existence. These defenses against anxiety likewise prevent the occurrence of the activities originally instigated by the impulse. The essence of repression lies in the elimination from consciousness of all ideas or memories that might help to arouse the impulse and thus reactivate the painful anxiety.

In his first descriptions of repression, Freud used the term "unpleasant" to describe the kinds of mental content that are subject to repression. This term was an unfortunate choice because of its wider meanings. Actually the anxiety that is fundamental to repression is that which was originally created by parents in punishing strongly motivated behavior. Such punishment helps to create the conscience, and when something re-arouses the anxiety later, the person may be said to suffer a threat of the loss of love.

Freud distinguished two kinds of repression, primal repression and after-expulsion. The description above is of the former. This elimination of impulses, however, is an active inhibitory process and other ideational contents or memories that are entirely unrelated to the repressed impulse can undergo *after-expulsion* if they are associated with the primal repression according to the ordinary laws of association. This is *repression proper,* and Freud considered that the majority of lacunae in the recall of unpleasant guilt-inducing and shameful memories was dependent on this rather than on a primal repression. Freud's best technical account of repression is in (1915b) and (1915c); a detailed and critical analysis of the concept, and of Freud's various related hypotheses, has been given by Sears (1936a).

INFANTILE AMNESIA

The earliest primal repressions are those of infancy. According to Freud (1905, pp. 36-38), the expression of both genital and pregenital impulses is met with disapproval from parents, and hence adult efforts at recall of early sexual experiences fail. A partial amnesia is created. By the process of repression proper, i.e., by a kind of associative amnesia, most of the other experiences of the preschool years are also obliterated.

It is true that most people have scanty memories for their early years, but there is no non-analytic evidence to support the notion that repression is responsible. Indeed, the data relating to the memorial process in infancy and to the recall of childhood memories by adults lead to quite the opposite conclusions; other factors are not only of demonstrable significance, but seem to be sufficient to account for the observed facts without postulating repression at all.

Careful studies by Dudycha and Dudycha (1933a, 1933b)

have shown that many college students are able to recall experiences from the third year. The average age at the time of the first remembered experience was 3 years, 7 months and the latest "first memory" was from the fifth birthday. A review by these authors (1941) of several other studies of childhood memories indicates that recollection of incidents from the third to the fifth year is normal for most adolescents and adults. There has been no comparison of the frequency of memories from various ages but the fact that the age of earliest memory is a research problem and that many people can recall only a few incidents from early life suggests that there is relatively poorer recall the farther back one goes in the life history. But there is in no sense any evidence of a general or complete amnesia, and the studies of Bell (1902) and Hamilton (1929) show that many adults are able to recall the details of childhood love affairs as well as other matters.

The emotions involved in such childhood memories include sexual ones accompanied by a realization of the forbidden character of the experience, anger, fear, wonder, awe, joy, shame and jealousy. Dudycha and Dudycha (1933a) report that approximately 40 per cent of 200 well authenticated memories involved fear. Some of these were fear of punishment for acknowledged misbehavior, and others were fear of animals or injury when the child's own behavior was not relevant. These authors do not report any memories of sex activity but the reports were not obtained under such conditions as might elicit such memories.

The evidence that factors other than repression are responsible for the relatively scanty recall from infancy has been well summarized by Brooks (1937, pp. 221-231). In order for an apparent decrement or deficiency of recall to be called an amnesia (loss of memory), there must be adequate evidence that the response was originally learned; the explanation of infantile amnesia, of course, assumes this. To Freud, impressed by the evident vividness of children's experiences, it seemed a truism that early emotional experiences were as well learned as the later ones of adults. This naive assumption has long since been blasted. The fact is that no matter how the process of memorizing during infancy is measured, there is clear proof that it is far below the efficiency of that of the older child or adult. Among the kinds of memory that have been studied have been recognition memory for pictures, recall memory for movements, rote memory for concrete and abstract words, for series of digits, for nonsense syllables and for poetry. In every instance the memorizing process has proved to be poor at the earliest level and to increase by a fairly constant rate to a later period. This relative inadequacy of the memorizing process, in other words, appears to parallel the relative inadequacy of recall for infantile experiences.

Crook and Harden (1931) reasoned, however, that if repression produced a general decrement in recall for the infancy period, there ought to be a positive relationship between the amount of amnesia and the amount of adult neuroticism. Child (1940) has aptly pointed out that this argument depends in part on two assumptions that are indefensible: that neuroticism and infantile repression are closely related, and that infantile amnesia is primarily a function of repression. The latter is demonstrably false and the former does violence to Freud's own reservations. Crook and Harden measured neuroticism with the Pressey X-O test and secured, by questionnaire, two measures of infantile amnesia: the age at earliest memory and the total number of memories from the preschool years. Correlations of —.37 and +.52 were obtained, respectively, between neuroticism and number of memories and between neuroticism and age at time of first recalled experience. These results appear to give a little support to the hypothesis, but only 19 subjects were used and the reliability and validity of the Pressey X-O test are so poor for this purpose that the results seem of little significance.

Child repeated the experiment with 290 subjects, using the Thurstone Personality Schedule, the Clark Revision of the Schedule, and the Bernreuter Personality Inventory with various subgroups. He found zero correlations between the measure of neuroticism and both measures of infantile amnesia. Further, the correlation between number of early memories and age at earliest recalled experience was only —.36. If these are measures of the same thing, they do not appear to be very reliable.

There is no good evidence, then, 1) that there is a sharply delimited infantile amnesia, 2) that the generally poor recall of childhood experiences requires other explanation than that of poor learning, or 3) that amount of infantile memory deficiency is related to adult neuroticism as this latter is measured by objective test procedures.

A word needs to be said, however, concerning the investigation of childhood memories. The marked influence of hypnosis on the recovery of memories suggests that strength of motivation is an important determiner of the amount and accuracy of recall from real life experiences (Stalnaker and Riddle, 1932; White, Fox and Harris, 1940). Exceptional care must be taken to avoid falsification of memory; so far no investigation has validated objectively the early occurrences subjects report. Undoubtedly, too, the stimulus constellation used for eliciting memories is important; recalls obtained in a classroom cannot be compared with those from the analytic couch or even from the quiet retrospection of a person who actively seeks his memories.

In psychoanalysis, the continuous harping on recall, the

demand to go farther back, to bring up more recollections, can be so harassing as to leave an objective observer in considerable doubt over the validity of the recalled items. (Cf. Landis, 1940.) And yet without such effort, one can scarcely feel confidence in the completeness of recall; certainly the non-analytic studies have so far been much too little concerned with the conditions of recall to be of importance in connection with the problem of repression. There is serious need of a theoretical as well as experimental evaluation of the whole technique of free association as a method of securing recall data.

MEASUREMENT OF REPRESSION

1. *The nature of the unpleasant.* Research on feeling and memory has been stimulated largely by the concept of repression. Freud dwelt at length on the obliviscence of the unpleasant and, because experimental psychologists could measure both hedonic tone and recall, the testing of this proposition has been often attempted. Unfortunately, a goodly proportion of the investigators have not inquired too closely into the meaning of the word "unpleasant" and much of the research that involves the relation of P and U feeling to memory is completely irrelevant to the problem of repression. (Cf. Sears, 1936a, pp. 255-257.)

Here is the reason. There are many kinds of "unpleasant" mental content, but the kinds that initiate the repression process are rather narrowly limited. These are the ones associated with anxiety arising from interference either with the conscience (or other motives designed to preserve the parents' love), or with the maintenance of pride and self-esteem. It was through the internalization of the punitive and restrictive attributes of the parents, and the threat of the loss of love, that the repression sequence was initiated. But, by and large, parents punish only those kinds of behavior that are contraindicated by their particular culture. In Western European and American cultures, for example, infantile as well as adolescent sex behavior is one of the most consistently punished forms of action, and hence sex is one of the most frequent sources of repression. Other motives that meet with vigorous socializing control are aggression, mastery, selfishness or egoism, and religious heterodoxy. As a consequence these motives and their ideational representations are peculiarly subject to repression. In addition, of course, each individual's parents have their own noncomformist specialties for the rearing of their children, and hence repressions may be created in connection with almost any impulse.

This situation should make it clear that when Freud refers to the "unpleasant" he is referring to ideas or memories that relate specifically to these kinds of motives and not to words, odors or pictures that for purely esthetic reasons have taken on the character of relative unpleasantness in the adult verbal system of thinking. Indeed, many memories and external stimuli that might be rated as definitely P by an adult may well have been indirectly associated with experiences of punishment in childhood—e.g., songs, perfumes, risqué stories and such words as *kiss, love* and *romance*. They would therefore be capable of eliciting guilt or anxiety and, possibly, repression. It must be kept in mind, then, that repression would be expected to occur with reference only to those ideas associated with impulses that come into conflict with the conscience (internalized punitive attributes of the parents) and not to ideas adjudged unpleasant on some other grounds. For this reason no consideration need be given here to the literature on the comparative recallability of P and U words, odors or nonsense syllables.

2. *Recall of experiences.* Of somewhat greater relevance to the theory is the group of studies designed to measure

recall of real life experiences. With these there is the possibility of securing memory material that does relate to the kinds of anxiety-induced unpleasantness to which repression theory refers.

The first study of this kind was that of Wohlgemuth (1923). Following a vacation period, he had 687 children from 11 to 16 years of age record their most pleasant and most unpleasant experiences of the preceding holidays. The task was repeated 10 days and 14 days later. The proportion of experiences forgotten was the same for both kinds but these findings are of little importance. The social conditions of the school, with a headmistress present at the experiment, made it doubtful that the children would reveal the kinds of shameful experiences to which the theory is applicable. Furthermore, the pleasant experiences were described first on each occasion and the relative amount of proactive and retroactive inhibition are unknown. The recalls, too, were not only recalls of the experiences but also of the previous written recalls.

Other experiments have uniformly found that recall of the pleasant experiences was better than of the unpleasant. (Cf. Moore, 1935.) In all cases, however, the technique of recall permitted some doubt as to just what was being recalled, the original experience or the description of it. Meltzer (1930) secured memories of all Christmas vacation experiences from 132 college students and these were rated as P and U. Recall was better for the former on the occasion of an unexpected test six weeks later. As was the case with studies by Jersild (1931), Menzies (1935), and Waters and Leeper (1936), there is no indication that truly repressible experiences were being described in the first place. This is perhaps less true of the study by Stagner (1931). He reports that the U experiences given by his subjects, college students, were mostly ones involving conflict. This does not guarantee their relevance but seems to put them closer to the type described by Freud. Stagner had his hundred subjects give but a single experience of each kind, and in connection with each, a list of "redintegrative items" such as colors, odors, and sounds that had been in some way associated with the original experience. Three weeks later he returned typewritten descriptions of the experiences to the subjects and required them to fill in the redintegrative items. There was a small but reliable difference in favor of better recall for the pleasant.

Perhaps the most realistic setting for this kind of experiment was that used by Koch (1930), who tested college students for the recall of school grades. She gave 10 quizzes during the early part of a semester and on each occasion the students rated the obtained grade on a scale of 1 to 5, the former being very satisfactory and the latter very unsatisfactory. The papers were collected again and 5 weeks after the last quiz the students were asked to recall all 10 grades. The "1" grades were best recalled, and whether "2" or "5" grades were second best for a particular person seemed to depend on the importance of a *bad* grade to the student, i.e., whether it was simply undesirable or constituted a real threat. In the latter case it was better remembered than the "2" grades. These results support the repression hypothesis but they show that relevance of the memory material to the immediate adjustment situation is also important in determining effectiveness of recall.

3. *Associative repression (after-expulsion).* A different method of tapping real-life repressions is exemplified in studies by Sharp (1930) and Flanagan (1930). Sharp constructed lists of paired associates that were meaningless so far as each member of the pair was concerned but suggested religious or profane meanings when pronounced together, as for example:

jeh–sus, tuw–hel, dah–mit. The rate of learning and the immediate and delayed recall of these lists were compared with those of control lists containing neutral words, as for example: mih–ten, muf–ler, res–ler. Flanagan used the same technique but his experimental list gave sexual meanings (tew–bal, piy–nis) and his control gave rural (gob–bal, har–nis). In both experiments the control lists were more quickly learned and were better recalled after 24 hours than were the experimental lists. All the differences were highly reliable.

The assumption involved in these experiments is that the words having salacious or profane or religious meanings had been associated, at some time in the subjects' lives, with experiences and ideas subject to repression. By associative transfer of this repressive inhibition, these words would then be inhibited also, and the learning would be slower and recall poorer than for similar paired associates that did not evoke associative inhibition. The results affirm the theoretical expectation, but the conditions under which the experiments were performed did not preclude the possibility that the differences was caused by embarrassment and conscious reluctance to speak forbidden words in the presence of the experimenter.

This difficulty was somewhat overcome in a later study by Sharp (1938). She obtained the case histories of a group of neurotic patients and from them selected fifteen words that referred to sources of anxiety and maladjustment for all the patients. These words were then formed into lists of paired associates by using present participles, as for example: feeling inferior, going insane, avoiding passion. A control list of words that related to gratifications was also secured. Experimental and control groups of patients required approximately the same number of trials to learn the two lists, but on recall tests after 2 days and again after 3 weeks, the unacceptable words were reliably less well recalled than the acceptable ones. Sharp secured similar results with the same lists from a group of normal adults enrolled in special classes.

Since the same words were used with the normals as with the neurotics, it seemed probable that the words were tapping some sources of repression that are fairly common in people with an American background. L. B. Heathers and Sears (1943) therefore attempted to repeat the experiment with another group of normal subjects similar in scholastic and general background to Sharp's group of normals. Neither with this group, however, nor with college students were differences in recall between the two lists obtained. A number of variations in procedure were introduced but none influenced the negative findings. Whatever may have been the source of the differences between the two sets of data, it seems probable that this method is too uncertain and unreliable for extensive investigation.

EXPERIMENTAL INDUCTION OF REPRESSION

The relative difficulty of measuring repressions that develop in the course of ordinary living has stimulated some effort to establish repression by artificial means in the laboratory. In an extensive exploratory study, Huston, Shakow and Erickson (1934) took advantage of the control over verbalization provided by hypnotic amnesia to create by suggestion the kinds of emotional conflict that would eventuate in repression or other mechanisms of conflict resolution. Under hypnosis, subjects were persuaded to believe things about themselves that caused embarrassment or shame. Amnesia was then suggested for the trance events. The investigators then brought up for discussion, either in conversation or by requesting appropriate actions, the matters that had been put into a conflict context under hypnosis. Little that was immediately relevant to repression was observed, but the technique of the experiment could well lend itself to intensive study of this problem.

Another repression producing technique, the significance of which cannot immediately be evaluated, has been proposed by McGranahan (1940). He constructed a list of 100 stimulus words which included 20 or more that were normally effective in producing free associations of colors, as for example: coal (black), butter (yellow). The list was presented to two groups of college students. One group was given no special instructions and the men were simply asked to write down their associations; this was done in a group. The members of the other group were taken individually and were instructed not to give color associations to any stimulus word; if they disobeyed they were to receive a very severe shock. The degree to which each subject broke down on a pursuit-meter when shocks were administered was also measured.

McGranahan found that the threat of shock was ineffective with some subjects and they persisted in giving color associations. The S. D. of the shock group was even larger than that of the control. The degree to which the subjects were able to "repress" the color associations in the experimental group correlated +.69 (rho) with their resistance to shock on the pursuit-meter test as measured by lack of disruption of the task. McGranahan concluded that the ability to repress was a function of cognitive organization.

The small number of subjects, coupled with the rather startling indication of a lack of inhibitory effect of threatened punishment, suggested the desirability of a further analysis of the experimental situation. Sears and Virshup (1943) presented the same list of stimulus words to three groups of 25 subjects each. All subjects were tested individually and care was taken to keep all the procedure, except that which was experimentally varied, as similar as possible for all groups. One group was a control; nothing was said about color responses. A second group was simply instructed not to give colors as associations. The third group, intended to be the same as McGranahan's experimental group, was warned not to give colors and was threatened with shock; subjects were given several samples of the shock in advance. The subjects of the control group gave colors without hesitation but neither of the other groups resembled McGranahan's. Both instructions and threatened shock reduced color associations somewhat, on the average, and there was no difference between the three groups in the size of the S. D. of the distribution of number of color responses given. This failure to reproduce the previous experimental results may have been a function of weaker shock, different instructions or some more intangible factor.

In order to secure a more accurate indication of the strength of the response words that were given by Groups 2 and 3, in place of the otherwise to be expected color associations, Sears and Virshup had the subjects return after 48 hours for a recall test of the responses given to the 100 stimulus words. It was found that with respect to the 20 words having *least frequent* color associations, as determined from the control groups, there were no differences between the 3 groups, but that with respect to the 20 words having *most frequent* color associations, again as determined from the control group, twice as many responses were forgotten in Groups 2 and 3 as in Group 1. This can be interpreted in either of two ways: that the "second choices" (instead of color) were not so strongly attached to the stimulus words, i.e., had not so much prior practice, and were therefore less well recalled, or that the inhibition produced either by instruction or threat of punishment prevented the recall. Since the interpretation is

ambiguous and McGranahan's results are not easily repro-
ducible, this general method of approach to the problem of
repression seems to have little to recommend it at present.

Of more immediate relevance is the study of Rosenzweig
and Mason (1934), who created anxiety in children by making
them fail at a semicompetitive laboratory task and then tested
for recall of the details of the task. The 40 children were
taken individually and given a series of rather simple jigsaw
puzzles. Before each puzzle was presented, the child was shown
a picture of how it would look when completed. Different
lengths of time were allowed for the different puzzles on the
pretext that they were of unequal difficulty. But the child
was permitted to finish only half the puzzles and it was suggested that he had "failed the test" on the others. The actual
amount of time allowed on the completed and uncompleted
puzzles was the same. After the series was finished the child
was asked to recall the names of all the puzzles he had tried.
In spite of the fact that the Zeigarnik effect would favor recall
of the uncompleted puzzles, these were less well remembered
than the completed ones.

There was additional evidence that it was the success and
failure that created the discrepancy in recall scores. The authors obtained from teachers ratings of the children on the
trait of "pride." Although these were none too reliable and
the differences were not great enough to furnish critical
proof, those children who rated high on pride did show a
greater tendency to forget the failed puzzles than did the
children who were rated low on pride. This suggests that the
interference with self-esteem was the significant variable in
relation to the forgetting.

Rosenzweig (1940) added further weight to this conclusion
with an experiment on Harvard students. He presented puzzles under two different conditions. In one case the students

were told that their intelligence was to be tested, and in the other that information concerning the relative difficulty of the puzzles was being sought. The first group was ego-involved in the situation and the second group was not. As would be predicted from the results of the previous experiment, there was greater recall of completed tasks in the ego-involved group and of uncompleted tasks in the other. In other words, the Zeigarnik effect was operative in the latter but was overcome by the selective recall of ego-maximating experiences in the former.

Various investigators have shown that artificially induced experiences of success and failure create sharp changes in the motivational and recall aspects of the learning process, and since the technique is one that lends itself readily to the laboratory, it would seem to offer considerable prospective reward to further investigation. Whether the more elaborate amnesic phenomena can be studied in such a setting is an open question, but at least the rudiments of repression may exist there. Rosenzweig's obtained differences have been relatively small, but larger groups and more refined techniques might remedy that, and hence permit investigation of the quantitative problems that Freud has already posed. (Cf. Sears, 1936a, pp. 253-255.) In any case, there seem to be no alternative techniques, to date, that give as much promise with the possible exception of induced emotional conflicts under hypnosis. The recall of real-life experiences does not permit manipulation of the variables that cause repression, except as there is a natural variation among different subjects, and the same holds true of the tapping of associative repressions (after-expulsion). With the latter technique, too, each subject must be treated with individual attention to his particular complexes and that makes quantification difficult.

CONCLUSIONS

There is little to be concluded from the experimental study of repression. In general it is possible to demonstrate that, with the required conditions crudely established, recall of either real-life or experimentally induced experiences follows the expectations suggested by repression theory. But the non-analytic data offer no refinement of the theory, no addition of relevant new variables, no streamlined techniques that promise eventual solution of the problems posed by Freud. Studies of recall of real-life experiences and efforts to tap existing repressions have been almost uniformly uninformative. Some hope may be held out for the artificial creation of repressions in the laboratory, but even these must by necessity be mild and impermanent. Indeed, the triviality of obtained differences in this field makes a most discouraging picture; and the coarseness of the experimental methods so far available for trapping the sensitive dynamics of repression does not augur well for the future.

Chapter VII

Projection and Dreams

PROBABLY the most inadequately defined term in all psychoanalytic theory is *projection*. Freud's original usage (1911) related to a defense mechanism whereby the qualities of one's own personality were perceived as being in someone else rather than the self. This served to defend the self against anxiety arising from impulses that are inescapably present but are forbidden.

Other usages have been implied, however, in connection with the development of the child's differentiation of himself from his environment, and with the so-called "projective techniques" for personality analysis. In the latter case the implication is that the motivational and organizational properties of a personality influence the perceptual and judgmental processes. This scarcely bears questioning, but such a usage must be separated from the defensive meaning given the term in the theory of paranoia.

MOTIVATIONALLY DETERMINED PERCEPTION

It may be said, in general, that the presence of a need or drive provides the antecedent condition for the perception of objects related to that need or drive. This has been exemplified by two significant experiments, one by Murray (1933) on anxiety and one by Sanford (1936, 1937) on hunger. Murray created an experimental situation in which anxiety was aroused, and obtained quantitative measures, before and after, of the degree to which the environment was perceived as fear-inducing. His subjects were five 11-year-old girls. The experiment was performed at a house party. In the evening Dr. Murray suggested a game of *murder*. At noon that day, each girl had rated 15 photographs of people, taken chiefly from *Time,* on a 9-point scale of kindness-maliciousness. Immediately after the exciting game they rated them again as well as 15 new pictures. The following noon they rerated the second set. Murray calculated the average rating attributed to the 30 photographs under the "noon and calm" and the "night and *murder*" conditions and found that 3 of the 5 girls rated them as reliably more malicious under the latter condition. The other 2 girls were more phlegmatic and did not change their average ratings. These individual differences were entirely consistent with other evidences of diffuse fearfulness exhibited at the house party during the remainder of the evening and the next morning.

Sanford's experiments exemplified essentially the same principle but added a quantitative principle of some importance. He presented incomplete pictures to college student subjects and asked them to say what kind of a scene the fragment was from, what had been taken away from the picture. Hungry subjects referred to food or other appurtenances of eating rather frequently, and by plotting the frequency of such references against the number of hours since the subject's last meal, Sanford was able to conclude that the frequency of eating completions was roughly a function of the duration of food deprivation.

IDEAS OF REFERENCE

One apparent example of this process is the behavior commonly called ideas of reference. This is the false perception of other people's noticing unduly or being derisively or contemptuously interested in the subject. Healy, Bronner and

Bowers (1930) ascribe this to the projection of feelings of self-criticism. An experimental demonstration of the behavior itself was given by Coover (1913) in connection with a study of alleged telepathic capacities. He tested the accuracy with which blindfolded subjects could tell whether or not they were being stared at from behind. The 10 subjects averaged 53 per cent guesses that they were being stared at and only 3 of the 10 made more "no" judgments than "yes." Coover concluded from the subjects' introspections that the feeling of being stared at came from "attributing an objective validity to commonly experienced subjective impressions in the form of imagery, sensations and impulses." One girl reported that she made "yes" judgments when she had a "feeling of being criticized" or a "feeling of nearness to the experimenter" and a "no" judgment when she had a "feeling of being alone." This reflects the connection between self-criticism and ideas of reference that has been observed clinically.

In order to get a more accurate measure of this relationship, Sears (1937a) constructed questionnaire scales for both ideas of reference and feelings of self-criticism. The items for the I-R scale contained such questions as these: Do you sometimes suspect that people on the street are laughing at you? Do other students seem to avoid sitting next to you in class? Do things often go wrong for you by no fault of your own? The following are items from the S-C scale: Do you often feel that you are a weakling in some ways? Do you ever have daydreams that make you ashamed of yourself? Are you worthy of the friendship of your associates?

In a group of nearly 300 college men, the scores of these two scales correlated +.82 when corrected for attenuation. Objective ratings of the social relations of some of these subjects were obtained from their friends; 2 to 5 men rated each of 123 of the men whose scores had been comparatively deviant from the average in some way, either by size or by discrepancy between the scores on the two scales. A comparison of these ratings with the subjects' statements about themselves showed that there was no objective validity of the ideas of reference.

These data verify the observations concerning a close relationship between false ideas that other people are behaving critically toward a subject and his own feelings of self-criticism. What the mechanics of the relationship are is not clear. In the case of some individuals who have an extreme discrepancy between the two variables there may be a defensive process present that involves repression. But in the majority of persons, whose scores on the two scales are approximately the same, there is no present reason for making such an assumption. It appears more likely that they simply perceive other people's behavior toward them as being consistent with their own evaluation of their own social stimulus value.

ATTRIBUTION OF TRAITS

Projection as a defense mechanism was first described in detail by Freud (1911) in connection with paranoia. Essentially the mechanism represented a displacement onto the outer world of traits, habits, attitudes or impulses that were characteristic of the subject himself. The projection was a defense against anxieties aroused by a knowledge of the existence of these qualities. In paranoia, for example, the delusions of persecution were supposed to be projections of the patient's own hatred of others, a hatred produced originally by reaction-formation from intolerable anxiety-evoking homosexual love impulses.

Such behavior is not susceptible of experimental manipulation and the two studies relating to this process have made use of selfish or stingy behavior, which is sufficiently tabooed to produce defensive reactions in those who exhibit it. The first of these (Sears, 1936b) has demonstrated the importance of *lack of insight* as an antecedent to projection. Sears secured self-ratings and ratings of each other from nearly 100 college men living in fraternities. The 7-point scales used were described as stinginess, obstinacy, disorderliness, and bashfulness. From these ratings it was possible, with each trait, to get a measure of the "true" amount of the trait possessed by the subject simply by averaging the ratings given him by his associates. A measure of the amount he attributed to others could be obtained by averaging his ratings of his associates. The correlations of these two variables were of negligible size but tended to be slightly negative.

By taking the factor of *insight* into account, however, it was shown that a projection mechanism was evidently operating in the judgment process. Insight was assumed to exist when a subject put himself in the same half of the distribution on a given trait in which his associates placed him. A comparison was made of the amount of each trait attributed to others by subjects who possessed and by those who lacked insight. These differences were not large, but they were all in the same direction and indicated that those who lacked insight had a greater tendency to project than did those who recognized the presence or absence of the trait in themselves.

Although this process appeared to operate with both the desirable and undesirable traits, e.g., with both stinginess and generosity, Posner (1940) found some evidence to indicate that feelings of guilt were of great importance in producing projection of selfishness. She created two social situations for eight-year-old children, one of which induced a feeling of guilt and the other not, and then measured the ensuing projection. Concretely, the situation was as follows: a child would be given two toys to play with, one of which he had previously indicated was highly preferred and the other of which was relatively nonpreferred. Then he was asked to give one of these toys to a friend to play with. After the choice was made, the child was asked which toy he thought the friend would have given away. By this procedure the child was first put in a conflict situation, the conflict being between his desire to keep the preferred toy and his desire to behave generously toward a friend. Having made a selfish choice (if he did), he would presumably feel guilty. The child's judgment about which toy the friend would have given away was the measure of projection; a selfish judgment (friend would give non-preferred toy) was considered projection. The control situation created to avoid guilt feelings did not include the request for the child himself to give away one of the toys; there was no conflict and no guilt. Posner found much less projected selfishness in the control than in the experimental group.

These two studies are roughly confirmatory of the proposition that projection occurs when a person is unwilling or incapable of making a true judgment about himself because of the painfulness of permitting such knowledge to come to consciousness. The confirmation is exceedingly indirect and the data are not without ambiguity, but they are at least susceptible of theoretical interpretation in terms of projection.

DREAMS

Freud's theory of the nature of dreaming (1900) is so complex that a review would be tedious. And, unhappily, the relevant objective data are so scanty that detailed reference to the theory would be useless. Non-analytic studies of dreams have been oriented, for the most part, toward description of the conscious or manifest content (e.g., Calkins, 1893; Bentley, 1915) and its classification into various kinds of psychological categories, such as fear, frustrated effort, wish fulfillment, etc. (e.g., Blanchard, 1926; Jersild, Markey and Jersild, 1933; Middleton, 1933; Gahagan, 1936; Witty and Kopel, 1939). Many of the facts elicited by these investigations are of major importance to any comprehensive theory of dreaming, but relatively few can be used for validation of Freud's hypotheses concerning the *interpretation* of dreams. Those that are relevant give fair support to the Freudian theories.

1. *Influence of external stimuli.* Among the factors that determine the manifest content of dreams, according to Freud, is the body of stimuli that impinge on the sleeper's sense organs. The role of these stimuli has been recognized by many investigators but little study has been made of them. Foster and Anderson (1936), in a survey of children's unpleasant dreams, found that the frequency of such dreams was positively related to the presence of others in bed or sleeping room, and possibly this can be interpreted as a generally stimulating influence from extrinsic sources.

More direct evidence was secured by Klein (1930) in a study of hypnotically induced dreams. Klein hypnotized his subjects and instructed them that they would dream and that they must report the dream at once to him. He then presented various rather sharply defined stimuli to the subjects, such as sounds, cold touch, cotton touch, and loss of support of the head. In each case it was possible to identify the influence of the external stimulus on the dream content, although the total content was by no means explicable solely in terms of the stimulus. In some instances the stimulus, e.g., a bell, did not appear until the very end of the described content of the dream, a whole incident having apparently been worked out by the dreamer to "explain" the sound. As Welch (1936) has shown, a vast amount of experience and many incidents can be compressed into a few rapidly following images, and evidently the incorporation of external stimuli can be managed

in such a way as to permit an explanatory image to precede
the representation of the stimulus in the dream. Needless to
say, the external stimuli used by Klein were disguised in the
manifest content of the dream.

Klein found that falling dreams, normally most common
among young adolescent boys (Jersild, Markey and Jersild,
1933), could be induced by loss of head support, and Horton
(1919, 1920) has presented an ingenious interpretation of a
number of levitation dreams in terms of vasomotor reactions
to definable external stimuli occurring during sleep.

While Klein's data are based on hypnotic rather than sleeping dreams, and are none too extensive, they seem sufficient,
when taken with the innumerable examples obtained in clinical practice, to verify the supposition that external stimuli
can initiate dreams and be incorporated, even if disguised, in
the manifest content.

2. *Events of the previous day.* Another source of dream
content is to be found in experiences the dreamer had during
the day preceding the dream. Kimmins (1931) reports that
this influence is very marked in children's dreams, and Foster
and Anderson (1936) found that the majority of young children's unpleasant dreams came from exciting events or experiences of this sort. In a questionnaire study of the dreams
of 170 college students of both sexes, Middleton (1933) obtained statements from 51.2 per cent of his subjects that experiences of the previous day were "usually" present in their
dreams. The experiment of Malamud and Linder (1931)
cited below gives a neatly controlled demonstration of the
process in action.

3. *Influence of motives.* Of far greater importance than
either of the above notions, which were in no way original
with Freud, is the conception of the dream as a method of
wish fulfillment. Perhaps no other aspect of Freud's psycho-

logical theories has met with so much petulant and uninformed ridicule as this. Academic psychologists whose sense of scholarship would be outraged by an inaccurate report of a theory of learning have boldly criticized Freud for ignoring the unpleasant character of anxiety dreams, for insisting that all dreams relate to sex, and for saying that all dreams involve disguise and distortion. Even a casual reading of but the first two chapters of *The Interpretation of Dreams* would have prevented such folly.

Boiled down to acceptable terminology, the wish fulfillment hypothesis becomes a statement that dreams are motivated. Freud was not accustomed to make the distinction between *efforts* to achieve gratification and the actual achievement itself; this was as true in the theories of sublimation and regression as in dreams. The dream was viewed as a *partial gratification,* at the phantasy level, having substitutive value for the true consummatory response. More than enough evidence has come from Lewin's laboratory (1935, pp. 190-191) to justify the assumption that phantasy can have such value. It was the presence of strivings toward gratification that Freud used as a criterion of "wish fulfilment."

A number of studies have reported group differences in the manifest content of both children's and adults' dreams. These differences are related to differences in strength of important motives, and serve as evidence that the content of dreams is largely determined by this factor.

Kimmins (1931) made a detailed content analysis of thousands of dreams individually reported by London school children of all ages and social conditions. A comparison of the dreams of children from industrial schools with those of regular school children living at home revealed sharp differences. The dreams of the former were almost wholly organized around home life. These institutionalized youngsters were from bad homes and broken homes; in contrast with children in normal homes, their desires for home life, visits from parents, and receipt of parcels from home would be expected to be stronger. The dream contents reflected this difference.

Similar data were obtained by Selling (1932), who questioned 200 boys about their dreams during the first week after they had entered a reformatory. He found that 80 per cent of the boys dreamed about home, mostly in connection with normal household routines, and that this subject represented the commonest content of their wishful phantasy during waking hours. Selling reports no control data on noninstitutionalized boys, but this figure is far higher than any obtained by Jersild, Markey and Jersild (1933) or Blanchard (1926), whose subjects were noninstitutionalized.

Other comparisons were made by Jersild, Markey and Jersild. These investigators made a survey, by a careful individual interview technique, of the dreams, fears and wishes of 400 public and private school children whose ages ranged from 5 to 12. There were 25 children of each sex at each year age level. Records of 1173 dreams were obtained.

Age and sex differences in the frequency of various kinds of dreams suggest that the contents are relevant to the kinds of motives and experiences most characteristic of each age and sex. Older children had more dreams about amusements, play and travel, and in the dreams suffered more frequently from embarrassment, guilt and social disapproval. Younger children had more magical happenings, fairies and angels, ghosts and bogey men. Boys more often dreamed about bodily injury and falling, and had more bad dreams about robbers, kidnappers, and about being powerless. Girls had more bad dreams about the loss of relatives. Children from the public school had more frankly wishful dreams about food, clothes, toys and other material objects, while the private school children (presumably of higher economic status) had more dreams about nonmaterial benefits. Most of the age and sex difference findings have been verified in a somewhat similar study by Witty and Kopel (1939), who examined an economically homogeneous group of Evanston school children.

In the Jersild study there was some indication that bad dreams were more closely related to the children's reported fears than to the unpleasant experiences they reported having had. This is further support for the general principle that motivation is of supreme importance, since the fears relate to situations the child still has to cope with and from which he wants to escape.

One experimental study of the influence of motives has been reported. Malamud and Linder (1931) and Malamud (1934) made careful examination of the case histories of a number of neurotic and psychotic patients and picked out for each one a central emotional problem. In order to discover whether an experience that was intimately related to this problem would be reflected in a subsequent dream, the experimenters exposed a small picture to the patient for 30 seconds, then asked for a description of it from memory. The pictures used for different patients were carefully selected to be relevant to each patient's emotional problem; for example, a man with a serious Oedipus complex was shown a print of the Madonna suckling a child. On the following morning the patient was asked to recall his dreams of the night before.

Malamud and Linder found that certain important items were always left out of the description that was given just after exposure, and that these apparently unnoticed items not infrequently would appear in some other context in the dreams of the subsequent night. Thus, in his memory description, the man with the Oedipus problem might not mention the fact that the child was actually at the breast, but such behavior would appear in another context in his reported dream.

The data of this experiment are not presented in statistical form and the complexity of the situation makes them difficult of interpretation. It does seem evident, however, that the content of these dreams was a function of experiences of the preceding day that were relevant to an important source of motivation.

CONCLUSIONS

Although the objective evidence at hand makes the presence of motivation in dreams unassailable, the importance of Freud's theory lies largely in the fact that it classes dreams with other orderly psychological phenomena. There is no aid to the interpretation of any particular dream in knowing that dreams are efforts at "wish fulfilment," and the theory does not even assist in distinguishing the antecedents of such diverse dream contents as nightmares and the undisguised wish fulfillments of young children. But useful or not, the theory is supported by the data. The kinds of dreams described by the various investigators serve, too, as a reminder that Freud did not limit all motivation to sex and that the first dream interpretation he published in detail was based on the motives of aggression, guilt reduction, and ego maximation (1900, Chapter 2).

Chapter VIII

Conclusions

PSYCHOANALYSIS is a science of personality. By the criteria of the physical sciences it is not a *good* science, but whatever its weaknesses it deals with many things other sciences have ignored, the development of forbidden impulses, the unconscious, a whole host of fantastic mechanisms of self-deceit. These aspects of human behavior can no longer be ignored; they must be incorporated into the general body of scientific knowledge. How to do this is a puzzler.

The experiments and observations examined in this report stand testimony that few investigators feel free to accept Freud's statements at face value. The reason lies in the same factor that makes psychoanalysis a bad science—its method. Psychoanalysis relies upon techniques that do not admit of the repetition of observation, that have no self-evident or denotative validity, and that are tinctured to an unknown degree with the observer's own suggestions. These difficulties may not seriously interfere with therapy, but when the method is used for uncovering psychological facts that are required to have objective validity it simply fails.

This does not mean that all psychoanalytic findings are false, but it does mean that other methods must be sought for their critical evaluation and validation. This present report has served as a summary of such efforts to date.

So, how much of psychoanalysis is "true"? Blunt as it may sound, this question is reasonable enough if it is interpreted to mean: how similar are the descriptions of personality development and operation that are given by the psychoanalytic method and by other methods of investigation? There can be no simple quantitative answer, of course, and there are no critical comparisons of the two kinds of personality description. It is possible to say only that certain facts do or do not support the theory. When a fact is said to support the theory nothing more is meant than that if the theory is true, the facts in question would be expected to exist. Nothing is implied about the *uniqueness* of the theory as an explanation of the facts—perhaps a dozen other theories would provide as good or better explanations—but the facts do not contravene the theory.

Still another consideration must be held in mind in trying to evaluate the degree of correspondence between the two sources of data: the nature of any fact is in part a function of the method by which it is obtained. The findings of psychoanalysis relate to the ideas and verbalizations that accompany various kinds of behavior, for example, sexual development. The data are secured from the free associations of adults, usually, and depend upon recall of childhood events. Like any other verbalizations about the experienced world, these communicate to others a picture of the world that cannot accord exactly with anyone's else; in other words, there are individualized distortions in the picture created by each person's unique language habits. Since the facts of psychoanalysis are derived entirely through verbal channels, allowance must be made for discrepancies that hinge mainly on the fact that non-analytic investigations frequently represent observations of other kinds of behavior.

This matter becomes very important in connection with such notions as the Oedipus complex. Freud assumed the Oedipus relationship to exist universally, and while other investigators have found instances of it, no indications of a universal cross-sex parental preference have been discovered in either children or adults. Is this discrepancy a function of the small and specialized sample of personalities in Freud's private practice, or is it a reflection of two different kinds of behavior samples, one a verbal recall by adults, the other a verbal affect judgment by children? Or what of the discrepancy between Freud's findings and Terman's? Both represent verbal recalls of childhood affections, but the methods of recall are very different, and Freud's explanation of such differences in terms of repression (Freud, 1920) cannot be independently validated.

In spite of these various difficulties and qualifications, a few conclusions relative to specific concepts and principles can be reached.

INFANTILE SEXUALITY

Freud's conception of infantile sexuality is rather well supported by other sources of information. The erotogenic character of the oral and anal-urethral zones has been established; children seek stimulation of these areas, interference with such behavior induces characteristic frustration reactions, and consummatory reactions appear to occur as the end of the activity. But there is no information on the degree to which this erotogeneity is native, although some cross-cultural comparisons suggest that practice at the securing of gratification increases the strength of the drive. There is no evidence, however, to confirm Freud's assumptions about the interrelationship between the various erotogenic zones. Whether one zone can serve as substitute for another is still undetermined. Evidence has been discovered, however, that certain conditions which might conduce to the development of such interrelationship do exist; in infancy there is frequent simultaneous activation of behavior centering around all three erotogenic zones.

Sexual behavior in childhood has been shown to be exceedingly common, and the so-called pregenital impulses give rise to exactly the same kinds of guilt and shame reactions (because they are forbidden) as do genital impulses. To this extent children may be said to be polymorphous perverse. There is no indication, however, that the castration complex is common. Quite the contrary. Children whose sex information is adequate show little tendency toward fears or curious beliefs about the sexual process. It seems probable that Freud's notions about children's attitudes toward sex were based on a small sample that was far from characteristic of contemporary American children.

OEDIPUS: A LESSON IN CULTURAL RELATIVITY

It is a truism today that adult behavior is a function of the culture in which it was learned. Psychiatric thought had not gone so far at the beginning of the century, however, and Freud's notion of the universal Oedipus complex stands as a sharply etched grotesquerie against his otherwise informative description of sexual development. From the analysis of data relating to object choice, it is apparent that in this matter perhaps more than in any other the nature of the chosen object and the reactions to other similar or dissimilar objects are dependent on the early home environment of the child. So far are we in agreement with Freud. But, beyond this, Freud seeks a common or typical pattern of development. If such existed, it could come only from a common culture pattern, i.e., from a constant situation in which learning could take place in a uniform way.

But there are no universal patterns of family life. Monogamy may be the legal marriage form, income tax laws may, by a system of exemptions, strongly reinforce the role of the mother as a child raiser and of the father as an income producer, and social custom may be so organized as to make difficult the lives of people who deviate from the standard culture pattern, but still there is only partial uniformity in family structure. Fathers die, or flee from their wives, or are constantly irritated, or become successful and absorbed in their work or unsuccessful and absorbed in their families— or vice versa. Mothers can differ in as many ways as fathers, and hence no two family situations are the same. Each one is to some extent unique *as a learning situation for the children.*

With this fact in mind it does not seem surprising that Freud's description of sexual development is inaccurate and incomplete. Furthermore, sex behavior is subject to such strong social control that it has become taboo in many of its forms in our own society. This factor probably serves to increase the variability of attitudes toward sex on the part of parents, and hence to add still another factor that creates variability in the conditions under which object choices and other aspects of sex behavior are learned.

The data from non-analytic sources include descriptions of sequences like those described by Freud; in other words, Freud was able to abstract one of the not too uncommon developmental patterns. But other sequences have been observed, too, and lead inescapably to the conclusion that Freud vastly underrated the importance of the child's immediate social milieu as a source for these kinds of learning, and overrated the uniformity of family patterns.

DEVELOPMENT AND REGRESSION: THE ROLE OF LEARNING

The psychoanalytic emphasis on life history is reflected in the non-analytic studies as a prepossession with the influence of learning. This interest applies principally in two connections—personality development and experimentally induced regression. In the case of the former there are few critical comparisons of different learning conditions that can be used to demonstrate the exact influence of rewards and punishments, although the nature of adult sexual distortions cries out for interpretation in such terms. In general it can be said that the objective data strongly reinforce the desirability of the life history approach so urgently required by psychoanalysis. The experimental studies of regression, however, have shown conclusively the necessity of dealing with this aspect of behavior in terms of a technically exact theory of learning.

In spite of the fact that virtually all the experimental work on regression has related to an aspect of that process that had been ignored by Freud, the general principles that have been discovered appear to apply equally well to the clinical varieties. Freud's supposition that fixation (strong habit) is the essential prerequisite for regression has been verified in detail by studies of the learning process in rats, and considerable light has been thrown on the conditions that predispose to greater habit strength. This same group of studies has also demonstrated, however, that frustration plays a less central role in regression than Freud had believed. It has proved to be simply an important one of several conditions that reduce the strength of ongoing habits and leave the way open for earlier fixations to produce regression. Two of these other conditions are satiation and alcohol.

These contributions from experimental animal psychology, involving conventional and highly exact laboratory techniques, appear to be the most fruitful of any of the objective studies of psychoanalytic phenomena. The reasons for this lie in a complex of factors. In the first place, fixation and regression relate to overt behavior to a far greater degree than do the majority of Freud's concepts; they are less susceptible, in other words, to the language confusions that arise from the psychoanalytic methods of investigation. Experimental psychology has become far better able to cope with such behavioral processes than with the more intangible thought processes represented by such concepts as repression and projection. Secondly, fixation and regression are part and parcel of the learning process, and of all the variegated phenomena that have interested psychologists, learning has been most extensively and successfully studied. In dealing with these two concepts, then, psychologists have had the relatively simple task of incorporating them into a vast and well charted body of facts and principles. As a corollary to this there is the fact that methods of investigation of learning are considerably more accurate and better understood than methods for studying any of the other phenomena of psychoanalysis.

MENTAL MECHANISMS

In contrast with the notable success of studies of fixation and regression, the work on the mechanisms of repression and projection has proved relatively unproductive. In each case there has been demonstration by non-analytic techniques that these processes exist and can be roughly measured. But in neither instance have the new methods of investigation been found to add appreciably to the available information. No new variables have been isolated and no new conditions of occurrence have been discovered. On the other hand, the fact of differential recallability for gratifying and anxiety-inducing experiences is of great importance, and the demonstrations of its existence (even with measurement by the coarse techniques of experimental psychology) lend some hope that future investigation may be more profitable. The same is true of projection, and in this case there is the additional satisfaction of knowing that Freud's suppositions about the importance of lack of insight and guilt feelings were correct.

Part of the reason for the unsatisfactory character of this research undoubtedly lies in the nature of the processes themselves. The so-called mental mechanisms are intangible processes at best. They are intimately related to both language and motivation, and in neither of these areas has experimental psychology yet developed either a sound systematic orientation or a body of technical information into which such concepts can easily be fitted. Also, the methods of experiment in these fields are less exact and less firmly embedded in theory than are the techniques for the study of the learning process.

Beyond these difficulties lies another, which is perhaps less easily overcome than these may be. Repression, projection and dreams are intimately dependent on strong emotions and motives. They are also dependent on language and verbal report. And these two dependencies taken together create difficulty in the laboratory. Strong emotion may safely be generated in animals, and nonemotional language or perceptual behavior may be studied in man. But animals are impossible reagents for the study of language, and the strong emotions cannot safely be used with man.

It appears that until some new conceptual organization of the facts from which these processes are inferred can be devised, progress in their investigation by non-analytic techniques must be slow.

THE DIRECTIONS OF PROGRESS

If psychoanalysis is viewed as a science of personality, there is reason to ask whether future research should follow in the same framework or whether some different theoretical orientation holds more promise. Such a question requires consideration of the use to which the science is to be put, of course. Two areas appear at present to cover the matter: one is education, conceived in the broadest sense; and the other is therapy or re-education. Psychoanalysis has been more or less successful at the latter task, but although Freud's influence has pervaded the mental hygiene movement, social work, child psychology and even the more formal aspects of education, there is little indication that the details of the theory have been widely used in formulating the details of educational practice. The kind of personality science that is more widely used in such work is *behavioral* rather than *experiential,* and since the behavioral way of thinking about personality is of even more recent origin than psychoanalysis, there seems good reason for concluding that a behavioral science of personality has been found more useful in the past and may be expected to be so in the future. In any case, the educative process deals directly with behavior rather than with consciousness or the unconscious, and presumably would find behavioral principles of more value than experiential ones.

The greater efficacy with which nonpsychoanalytic techniques deal with behavioral processes has already been sufficiently emphasized. It would seem desirable, therefore, that future research by such methods should be designed to aid in the development of a science of personality that is not structured along the same lines as psychoanalysis, but has a systematic structure of its own based on the triumvirate of influences loosely defined as *growth, learning,* and *the social milieu.*

From a research standpoint, the data that have been surveyed in this report suggest three kinds of investigatory effort that give outstanding promise of contributing richly to the development of such a science of personality.

First, there is crying need for the results of longitudinal research on personality development. Several projects have collected intimate and detailed data on the growing personalities of children, and some of these findings have been mentioned here. There are a great number of important hypotheses to be derived from psychoanalytic theory, however, that have not been tested with these data. Until such problems as the organization and interrelationships of pregenital impulses have been examined by reference to records obtained *year after year from the same child,* there are going to be serious lacunae in our knowledge of the motivational sources of adult sexuality and dependencies.

Second, the studies of object fixation, as well as of instrumental act fixation and regression, have pointed the way to fruitful research concerning the influence of learning on motivation. With little expense, and with virtually no waste motion on the development of new experimental techniques, a vastly significant contribution to the problem of secondary motivation could be made by animal psychologists.

Third, cross-cultural comparisons of personality development can assist in evaluating the significance of the social milieu as a source of motivational and trait characteristics. If the basic assumption of both psychoanalysis and behavioral personality science is correct, i.e., if the conditions of childhood learning largely determine adult characteristics, it is evident that the social milieu in which the child grows up is of pre-eminent significance in determining the nature of his secondary motives and his basic personality structure. Such problems as that of the influence of practice on strength of genital or pregenital impulses (cf. Chapter II) can be solved only by comparison of large groups which have received different opportunities for learning. Nowhere is it possible to secure such large differences in the experience of whole groups as in ethnological data of different culture groups. In a society that is a going concern, too, it is possible to be sure that *all* influences are directed to a given kind of training;

there is not the danger that specialized and controlled training in the laboratory or nursery school is constantly being nullified by a different (and normal to the culture) training program in the home. Likewise, children living in the culture are brought up in a way that is "normal" to that culture, whereas experimental groups (e.g., orphans, institutionalized children, etc.) are brought up as acknowledged deviants from their own society and hence this extra variable enters.

The suggestion of these three types of research does not argue against pure psychoanalytic research. Such research must be evaluated on other grounds, and the present report gives no basis for estimating its desirability. The present suggestions are designed to support the development of a science of personality that is behavioral in character. They reflect the general conclusion from this survey that other social and psychological sciences must gain as many hypotheses and intuitions as possible from psychoanalysis but that the further analysis of psychoanalytic concepts by nonpsychoanalytic techniques may be relatively fruitless so long as those concepts rest in the theoretical framework of psychoanalysis.

Bibliography

Achilles, P. S. (1923) The effectiveness of certain social hygiene literature. New York: Amer. Soc. Hyg. Assoc.

Barker, R., Dembo, T., and Lewin, K. (1941) Frustration and regression: an experiment with young children. *Studies in Topological and Vector Psychology II. Univ. Iowa Stud. Child Welf.*, 18, No. 1, 1-314.

Bell, S. (1902) A preliminary study of the emotion of love between the sexes. *Amer. J. Psychol.*, 13, 325-354.

Bentley, M. (1915) The study of dreams. *Amer. J. Psychol.*, 26, 196-210.

Billig, A. L. (1941) Finger nail-biting: its incipiency, incidence, and amelioration. *Genet. Psychol. Monogr.*, 24, 123-218.

Blanchard, P. (1926) A study of subject matter and motivation of children's dreams. *J. abn. (soc.) Psychol.*, 21, 24-37.

Blanton, M. G. (1917) The behavior of the human infant during the first thirty days of life. *Psychol. Rev.*, 24, 456-483.

Brogden, W. J. (1939) Higher order conditioning. *Amer. J. Psychol.*, 52, 579-591.

———— (1940) Retention of conditioned responses tested by experimental extinction. *Amer. J. Psychol.*, 53, 285-288.

Brogden, W. J., and Culler, E. (1935) Experimental extinction of higher-order responses. *Amer. J. Psychol.*, 47, 663-669.

Bromley, D. D., and Britten, F. H. (1938) Youth and sex. (A study of 1300 college students.) New York: Harpers.

Brooks, F. D. (1937) Child psychology. Boston: Houghton Mifflin.

Bugelski, R. (1938) Extinction with and without sub-goal reinforcement. *J. comp. Psychol.*, 26, 121-133.

Calkins, M. W. (1893) Statistics of dreams. *Amer. J. Psychol.*, 5, 311-343.

Cameron, N. (1938a) Reasoning, regression and communication in schizophrenics. *Psychol. Monogr.*, 50, No. 1.

———— (1938b) A study of thinking in senile deterioration and schizophrenic disorganization. *Amer. J. Psychol.*, 51, 650-664.

Campbell, E. H. (1939) The social-sex development of children. *Genet. Psychol. Monogr.*, 21, No. 4.

Child, I. L. (1940) The relation between measures of infantile amnesia and of neuroticism. *J. abn. (soc.) Psychol.*, 35, 453-456.

Commins, W. D. (1932) The marriage-age of oldest sons. *J. soc. Psychol.*, 3, 487-490.

Conn, J. H. (1939) Factors influencing development of sexual attitudes and sexual awareness in children. *Amer. J. Dis. Children,* 58, 738-745.

———— (1940) Children's reactions to the discovery of genital differences. *Amer. J. Orthopsychiat.,* 10, 747-754.

Coover, J. E. (1913) "The feeling of being stared at"—experimental. *Amer. J. Psychol.,* 24, 570-575.

Cowles, J. T. (1937) Food-tokens as incentives for learning by chimpanzees. *Comp. Psychol. Monogr.,* 14, No. 71.

Cowles, J. T., and Nissen, H. W. (1937) Reward-expectancy in delayed responses of chimpanzees. *J. comp. Psychol.,* 24, 345-358.

Crook, M. N., and Harden, L. (1931) A quantitative investigation of early memories. *J. soc. Psychol.,* 2, 252-255.

Davis, K. B. (1929) Factors in the sex life of twenty-two hundred women. New York: Harpers.

DuBois, P. H., and Forbes, T. W. (1934) Studies of catatonia. III. Bodily postures assumed while sleeping. *Psychiat. Quart.,* 8, 546-552.

Dudycha, G. J., and Dudycha, M. M. (1933a) Adolescents' memories of preschool experiences. *J. genet. Psychol.,* 42, 468-480.

———— (1933b) Some factors and characteristics of childhood memories. *Child Develpm.,* 4, 265-278.

———— (1941) Childhood memories: a review of the literature. *Psychol. Bull.,* 38, 668-682.

Duncker, K. (1938) Experimental modification of children's food preferences through social suggestion. *J. abn. (soc.) Psychol.,* 33, 489-507.

Elliott, M. H. (1928) The effect of change of reward on the maze performance of rats. *Univ. Calif. Publ. Psychol.,* 4, 19-30.

Ellson, D. G. (1938) Quantitative studies of the interaction of simple habits. I. Recovery from specific and generalized effects of extinction. *J. exp. Psychol.,* 23, 339-358.

Everall, E. E. (1935) Perseveration in the rat. *J. comp. Psychol.,* 19, 343-369.

Fairlie, C. W. (1937) The effect of shock at the 'moment of choice' on the formation of a visual discrimination habit. *J. exp. Psychol.,* 21, 662-669.

Fenichel, O. (1934) Outline of clinical psychoanalysis. New York: W. W. Norton.

Finan, J. L. (1940) Quantitative studies in motivation. I. Strength of conditioning in rats under varying degrees of hunger. *J. comp. Psychol.,* 29, 119-134.

Finch, G., and Culler, E. (1934) Higher order conditioning with constant motivation. *Amer. J. Psychol.,* 46, 596-602.

Flanagan, D. (1930) The influence of emotional inhibition on learning and recall. Unpublished Master's Thesis, Univ. of Chicago.

Fletcher, F. M. (1940) Effects of quantitative variation of food-incentive on the performance of physical work by chimpanzees. *Comp. Psychol. Monogr.*, 16, No. 82.

Foster, J. C., and Anderson, J. E. (1936) Unpleasant dreams in childhood. *Child Develpm.*, 7, 77-84.

Frenkel-Brunswik, E. (1939) Mechanisms of self-deception. *J. soc. Psychol.*, 10, 409-420.

Freud, S. (1900) The interpretation of dreams. (Third edition; translated by A. A. Brill). London: G. Allen and Unwin, 1919.

———— (1905) Three contributions to the theory of sex. (Fourth edition.) *Nervous and Mental Disease Monograph Series*, 1930, No. 7.

———— (1908) Character and anal erotism. *Collected Works*, 2, 45-50.

———— (1911) Psycho-analytic notes upon an autobiographical account of a case of paranoia (dementia paranoides). *Collected Papers*, 3, 387-470.

———— (1914) On narcissism: an introduction. *Collected Works*, 4, 30-59.

———— (1915a) Instincts and their vicissitudes. *Collected Papers*, 4, 60-83.

———— (1915b) Repression. *Collected Papers*, 4, 84-97.

———— (1915c) The unconscious. *Collected Papers*, 4, 98-136.

———— (1920) General introduction to psychoanalysis. New York: Boni and Liveright.

———— (1924) The passing of the Oedipus-complex. *Collected Works*, Vol. 2.

———— (1933) New introductory lectures on psycho-analysis. New York: Norton.

Gahagan, L. (1936) Sex differences in recall of stereotyped dreams, sleep-talking, and sleep-walking. *J. genet. Psychol.*, 48, 227-236.

Gardner, G. E. (1931) Evidences of homosexuality in 120 unanalyzed cases with paranoid content. *Psychoanal. Rev.*, 18, 57-62.

Granich, L. (1932) A systematic translation of psychoanalytic concepts. *J. abn. (soc.) Psychol.*, 27, 302-320.

———— (1935) A systematic translation of psychoanalytic concepts. II. The sex instinct and sublimation. *J. abn. (soc.) Psychol.*, 29, 390-396.

Halverson, H. M. (1938) Infant sucking and tensional behavior. *J. genet. Psychol.*, 53, 365-430.

———— (1940) Genital and sphincter behavior of the male infant. *J. genet. Psychol.*, 56, 95-136.

Hamilton, G. V. (1929) A research in marriage. New York: A. and C. Boni.

Hamilton, J. A., and Krechevsky, I. (1933) Studies in the effect of shock upon behavior plasticity in the rat. *J. comp. Psychol.*, 16, 237-253.

Hanks, L. M., Jr. (1940) An explanation of the content of dreams through an interpretation of dreams of convicts. *J. gen. Psychol.*, 23, 31-46.

Hattendorf, K. W. (1932) A study of the questions of young children concerning sex: a phase of an experimental approach to parent education. *J. soc. Psychol.*, 3, 37-65.

Healy, W., Bronner, A., and Bowers, A. M. (1930) The structure and meaning of psychoanalysis. New York: Alfred A. Knopf.

Heathers, G. L., and Arakelian, P. (1941) The relation between strength of drive and rate of extinction of a bar-pressing reaction in the rat. *J. gen. Psychol.*, 24, 243-258.

Heathers, L. B., and Sears, R. R. (1943) Experiments on repression. II. The Sharp technique. (In preparation.)

Henry, G. W., and Galbraith, H. M. (1934) Constitutional factors in homosexuality. *Amer. J. Psychiat.*, 90 (13), 1249-1270.

Horton, L. H. (1919) Levitation dreams: their physiology. *J. abn. Psychol.*, 14, 145-172.

———— (1920) How "stimulus-and-reaction" explains levitation dreams. *J. abn. (soc.) Psychol.*, 15, 11-35.

Hull, C. L. (1934) The rat's speed-of-locomotion gradient in the approach to food. *J. comp. Psychol.*, 17, 393-422.

Humphreys, L. G. (1939a) The effect of random alternation of reinforcement on the acquisition and extinction of conditioned eyelid reactions. *J. exp. Psychol.*, 25, 141-158.

———— (1939b) Acquisition and extinction of verbal expectations in a situation analogous to conditioning. *J. exp. Psychol.*, 25, 294-301.

Huston, P. E., Shakow, D., and Erickson, M. H. (1934) A study of hypnotically induced complexes by means of the Luria techniques. *J. gen. Psychol.*, 11, 65-97.

Isaacs, S. (1933) Social development in young children. London: George Routledge and Sons.

Jensen, K. (1932) Differential reactions to taste and temperature stimuli in newborn infants. *Genet. Psychol. Monogr.*, 12, 361-469.

Jersild, A. T. (1931) Memory for the pleasant as compared with the unpleasant. *J. exp. Psychol.*, 14, 284-288.

Jersild, A. T., Markey, F. V., and Jersild, C. L. (1933) Children's fears, dreams, wishes, daydreams, likes, dislikes, pleasant and unpleasant memories. New York: Bur. of Publ., T. C., *Child Develpm. Monogr.*, No. 12.

Jones, M. R. Studies in "nervous" movements: I. The effect of mental arithmetic on the frequency and patterning of movements. *J. gen. Psychol.* (in press).

Kimmins, C. W. (1931) Children's dreams. *In* Murchison, C., *Handbook of Child Psychology.* Worcester, Mass.: Clark Univ. Press. Pp. 527-554.

Kirkpatrick, C. (1937) A statistical investigation of the psychoanalytic theory of mate selection. *J. abn. (soc.) Psychol.*, 32, 427-430.

Klein, D. B. (1930) The experimental production of dreams during hypnosis. *Univ. Texas Bull.*, No. 3009.

Koch, H. L. (1930) The influence of some affective factors upon recall. *J. gen. Psychol.*, 4, 171-190.

—————— (1935) An analysis of certain forms of so-called "nervous habits" in young children. *J. genet. Psychol.*, 46, 139-170.

Krechevsky, I., and Honzik, C. H. (1932) Fixation in the rat. *Univ. Calif. Publ. Psychol.*, 6, 13-26.

Landis, C. (1940) Psychoanalytic phenomena. *J. abn. (soc.) Psychol.*, 35, 17-28.

Landis, C., Landis, A., Bolles M., *et al.* (1940) Sex in development. New York: Paul B. Hoeber.

Levy, D. M. (1928) Fingersucking and accessory movements in early infancy. *Amer. J. Psychiat.*, 7, 881-918.

—————— (1934) Experiments on the sucking reflex and social behavior of dogs. *Amer. J. Orthopsychiat.*, 4, 203-224.

—————— (1940) "Control-situation" studies of children's responses to the differences in genitalia. *Amer. J. Orthopsychiat.*, 10, 755-762.

Lewin, K. (1935) A dynamic theory of personality (trans. by D. Adams and K. Zener). New York: McGraw-Hill.

Macfarlane, J. W. (1939) The relation of environmental pressures to the development of the child's personality and habit patterning. *J. Pediat.*, 15, 142-152.

Malamud, W. (1934) Dream analysis. *Arch. Neurol. and Psychiat.*, Chicago 31, 356-372.

Malamud, W., and Linder, R. E. (1931) Dreams and their relationship to recent impressions. *Arch. Neurol. and Psychiat.*, 25, 1081-1099.

Malinowski, B. (1927) Prenuptial intercourse between the sexes in the Trobriand Islands, N.W. Melanesia. *Psychoanal. Rev.*, 14, 20-36.

Mangus A. R. (1936) Relationships between the young woman's conceptions of her intimate male associates and of her ideal husband. *J. soc. Psychol.*, 7, 403-420.

Martin, R. F. (1940) "Native" traits and regression in rats. *J. comp. Psychol.*, 30, 1-16.

McGranahan, D. V. (1940) A critical and experimental study of repression. *J. abn. (soc.) Psychol.*, 35, 212-225.

Mead, M. (1935) Sex and temperament. New York: William Morrow.

Meltzer, H. (1930) Individual differences in forgetting pleasant and unpleasant experiences. *J. educ. Psychol.*, 21, 399-409.

Menzies, R. (1935) The comparative memory values of pleasant, unpleasant and indifferent experiences. *J. exp. Psychol.*, 18, 267-279.

Middleton, W. C. (1933) Nocturnal dreams. *Sci. Monthly,* November, 460-464.

Mierke, K. (1933) Über die Objectionsfähigkeit und ihre Bedeutung für die Typenlehre. *Arch. ges. Psychol.,* 89, 1-108.

Miller, N. E. (1939) Experiments relating Freudian displacement to generalization of conditioning. *Psychol. Bull.,* 36, 516-517.

Miller, N. E., and Miles, W. R. (1936) Alcohol and removal of reward. *J. comp. Psychol.,* 21, 179-204.

Moore, E. H. (1935) A note on the recall of the pleasant vs. the unpleasant. *Psychol. Rev.,* 42, 214-215.

Mowrer, O. H. (1940) An experimental analogue of "regression" with incidental observations on "reaction-formation." *J. abn. (soc.) Psychol.,* 35, 56-87.

Murray, H. A., Jr. (1933) The effect of fear upon estimates of the maliciousness of other personalities. *J. soc. Psychol.,* 4, 310-329.

Nowlis, H. H. (1941) The influence of success and failure on the resumption of an interrupted task. *J. exp. Psychol.,* 28, 304-325.

O'Kelly, L. I. (1940a) An experimental study of regression. I. Behavioral characteristics of the regressive response. *J. comp. Psychol.,* 30, 41-53.

————— (1940b) An experimental study of regession. II. Some motivational determinants of regression and perseveration. *J. comp. Psychol.,* 30, 55-95.

Olson, W. C. (1929) The measurement of nervous habits in normal children. Minneapolis: Univ. of Minnesota Press.

————— (1936) The diagnosis of oral habits in children from the condition of the hands. *J. abn. (soc.) Psychol.,* 31, 182-189.

Page, J., and Warkentin, J. (1938) Masculinity and paranoia. *J. abn. (soc.) Psychol.,* 33, 527-531.

Peterson, R. C., and Thurstone, L. L. (1932) The effect of a motion picture film on children's attitudes toward Germans. *J. educ. Psychol.,* 23, 241-246.

Platonow, K. I. (1933) On the objective proof of the experimental personality age regression. *J. gen. Psychol.,* 9, 190-209.

Posner, B. A. (1940) Selfishness, guilt feelings and social distance. Unpublished Master's Thesis, Univ. of Iowa.

Pratt, K. C., Nelson, A. K., and Sun, K. H. (1930) The behavior of the newborn infant. *Ohio State Univ. Studies. Contributions in Psychology,* No. 10. Ohio State Univ. Press.

Razran, G. H. S. (1938a) Conditioning away social bias by the luncheon technique. *Psychol. Bull.,* 35, 693.

————— (1938b) Music, art, and the conditioned response. Paper, Eastern Psychological Association, April 1-2.

Rosenzweig, S. (1937) Personal communication.

——— (1938) The experimental study of repression. *In* Murray, H. A., *Explorations in personality.* New York: Oxford Univ. Press. Pp. 472-490.

——— (1940) Need-persistive and ego-defensive reactions to frustration as demonstrated by an experiment on repression. MS.

Rosenzweig, S., and Mason, G. (1934) An experimental study of memory in relation to the theory of repression. *Brit. J. Psychol.,* 24, 247-265.

Sackett, R. S. (1939) The effect of strength of drive at the time of extinction upon resistance to extinction in rats. *J. comp. Psychol.,* 27, 411-431.

Sanders, M. J. (1937) An experimental demonstration of regression in the rat. *J. exp. Psychol.,* 21, 493-510.

Sanford, R. N. (1936) The effects of abstinence from food upon imaginal processes: a preliminary experiment. *J. Psychol.,* 2, 129-136.

——— (1937) The effects of abstinence from food upon imaginal processes: a further experiment. *J. Psychol.,* 3, 145-159.

Sears, R. R. (1936a) Functional abnormalities of memory with special reference to amnesia. *Psychol. Bull.,* 33, 229-274.

——— (1936b) Experimental studies of projection: I. Attribution of traits. *J. soc. Psychol.,* 7, 151-163.

——— (1937a) Experimental studies of projection: II. Ideas of reference. *J. soc. Psychol.,* 8, 389-400.

———(1937b) Initiation of the repression sequence by experienced failure. *J. exp. Psychol.,* 20, 570-580.

——— (1941) Non-aggressive reactions to frustration. *Psychol. Rev.,* 48, 343-346.

——— (1943) Experimental analyses of psychoanalytic phenomena. *In* Hunt, J. McV., (ed.), *Fundamentals of personality and behavior disorders.* New York: Ronald Press.

Sears, R. R., and Virshup, B. (1943) Studies of repression: III. The McGranahan method. (In preparation.)

Selling, L. S. (1932) Effect of conscious wish upon dream content. *J. abn. (soc.) Psychol.,* 27, 172-178.

Sharp, A. A. (1930) The influence of certain emotional inhibitions on leaning and recall. Unpublished Master's Thesis, Univ. of Chicago.

——— (1938) An experimental test of Freud's doctrine of the relation of hedonic tone to memory revival. *J. exp. Psychol.,* 22, 395-418.

Skinner, B. F. (1936) The effect on the amount of conditioning of an interval of time before reinforcement. *J. gen. Psychol.,* 14, 279-295.

Stagner, R. (1931) The redintegration of pleasant and unpleasant experiences. *Amer. J. Psychol.,* 43, 463-468.

Stagner, R., and Drought, N. (1935) Measuring children's attitudes toward their parents. *J. educ. Psychol.,* 26, 169-176.

Stalnaker, J. M., and Riddle, E. E. (1932) The effect of hypnosis on long-delayed recall. *J. gen. Psychol.,* 6, 429-440.

Stogdill, R. M. (1937) Survey of experiments of children's attitudes toward parents: 1894-1936. *J. genet. Psychol.*, 51, 293-303.

Stott, L. H. (1940) Adolescents' dislikes regarding parental behavior, and their significance. *J. genet. Psychol.*, 57, 393-414.

Strakosch, F. M. (1934) Factors in the sex life of seven hundred psychopathic women. Utica, N.Y.: State Hospitals Press.

Symonds, P. M. (1939) The psychology of parent-child relationships. New York: Appleton-Century.

Taylor, W. S. (1933) A critique of sublimation in males: a study of forty superior single men. *Genet. Psychol. Monogr.*, 13, No. 1.

Terman, L. M. (1938) Psychological factors in marital happiness. New York: McGraw-Hill.

Terman, L. M., and Miles, C. C. (1936) Sex and personality. New York: McGraw-Hill.

Thurstone, L. L. (1931a) The measurement of change in social attitude. *J. soc. Psychol.*, 2, 230-235.

———— (1931b) Influence of motion pictures on children's attitudes. *J. soc. Psychol.*, 2, 291-305.

Waters, R. H., and Leeper, R. (1936) The relation of affective tone to the retention of experiences of daily life. *J. exp. Psychol.*, 19, 203-215.

Wechsler, D. (1931) The incidence of significance of fingernail biting in children. *Psychoanal. Rev.*, 18, 201-209.

Welch, L. (1936) The space and time of induced hypnotic dreams. *J. Psychol.*, 1, 171-178.

Wells, F. L. (1935) Social maladjustments: adaptive regression. *In* Murchison, C., *Handbook of Social Psychology*. Worcester, Mass.: Clark Univ. Press, Chapter 18.

White, R. W., Fox, G. F., and Harris, W. W. (1940) Hypnotic hypermnesia for recently learned material. *J. abn. (soc.) Psychol.*, 35, 88-103.

Williams, K. A. (1929) The reward value of a conditioned stimulus. *Univ. Calif. Publ. Psychol.*, 4, 31-55.

Williams, S. B. (1938) Resistance to extinction as a function of the number of reinforcements. *J. exp. Psychol.*, 23, 506-522.

———— (1941a) Transfer of extinction effects in the rat as a function of habit strength. *J. comp. Psychol.*, 31, 263-280.

———— (1941b) Transfer of reinforcement in the rat as a function of habit strength. *J. comp. Psychol.*, 31, 281-296.

Willoughby, R. R. (1937) Sexuality in the second decade. *Monogr. Soc. Res. Child Developm.*, 2, No. 10.

Witty, P. and Kopel, D. (1939) The dreams and wishes of elementary-school children. *J. educ. Psychol.*, 30, 199-205.

Wohlgemuth, A. (1923) The influence of feeling on memory. *Brit. J. Psychol.*, 13, 405-416.

Wolfe, J. B. (1936) Effectiveness of token-rewards for chimpanzees. *Comp. Psychol. Monogr.,* 12, No. 60, 1-72.

Young, P. C. (1940) Hypnotic regression—fact or artifact? *J. abn. (soc.) Psychol.,* 35, 273-278.

Youtz, R. E. P. (1938) Reinforcement, extinction, and spontaneous recovery in a non-Pavlovian reaction. *J. exp. Psychol.,* 22, 305-318.

———— (1939) The weakening of one Thorndikian response following the extinction of another. *J. exp. Psychol.,* 24, 294-304.

Index

Achilles, P. S., 46
After-expulsion, 106, 113-115
Age regression, 98-100
Aggression, x, 23
Amnesia,
   hypnotic, 115-116
   infantile, 64, 106-110
Anal character, 67-70
Anderson, J. E., 127-128
Anxiety, 105-106, 110-111, 121-122
   dreams, 129-132
Arakelian, P., 89
Arapesh, 34-35

Barker, R., 77, 97-98
Bell, S., 44-45, 107
Bentley, M., 126
Billig, A. L., 10-11
Blanchard, P., 127, 130
Blanton, M. G., 3, 15
Bowers, A. M., 123
Britten, F. H., 64
Brogden, W. J., 86-87
Bromley, D. D., 64
Bronner, A., 122
Brooks, F. D., 107-108
Bugelski, R., 86

Calkins, M. W., 126
Cameron, N., 100
Campbell, E. H., 45-46
Cathexis, 78
   experimental control of, 55-57
Child, I. L., 108-109
Childhood experiences,
   recall of, 26-29, 111-113
Childhood love affairs, 44-45
Commins, W. D., 54
Conn, J. H., 30-31
Conscience, 105
Constipation, 15, 67
Coover, J. E., 123
Cowles, J. T., 79, 84
Crook, M. N., 108
Culler, E., 86-87
Culture,
   Arapesh, 34-35
   effect on behavior, 25-26, 29, 31,
     32, 35-37, 43, 46-47, 52, 57-58,
     136-137, 142-143

   middle-western, 45
   Trobriand Islands, 29, 35-36, 45

Davis, K. B., 41, 46, 64-65
Defecation, 20-21
Dembo, T., 77, 97-98
Detumescence (see Tumescence)
Dreams, 126-132
   external stimuli, 127-128
   hypnotic, 127-128
   influence of motives, 128-132
   manifest content, 126-128
   sex differences, 130
Drought, N., 43
DuBois, P. H., 102
Dudycha, G. J., 106-107
Dudycha, M. M., 106-107
Duncker, K., 56

Elliott, M. H., 80
Ellson, D. G., 88
Erection,
   penial, 15-17
Erickson, M. H., 115-116
Erotism,
   anal, 2, 14-15, 27, 63, 67-69
   autoerotism, 2, 9, 15, 39-41, 62, 64
   genital, 15-18
   oral, 2-13, 19-20, 24, 34-35
   urethral, 24-25, 27, 63
Erotogenesis, 1-22
Erotogenic zones, 1-2, 76
   interrelationships, 18-21, 25-26
Everall, E. E., 85
Exhibitionism, 25, 27, 44, 63
   sex differences, 63

Failure (see Success and Failure)
Fairlie, C. W., 85
Fenichel, O., 39, 59, 62, 100
Fetichism, 63, 68
Finan, J. L., 83, 93
Finch, G., 86
Fingersucking (see Pleasure-sucking)
Fixation, 76-96
   on clitoris, 59, 61-62
   definition, 81
   electric shock, 85-86
   habit strength, 78, 79, 81
   instrumental act, 81-89

interference effect of, 80-81
object, 77, 78-81
Flanagan, D., 113-114
Fletcher, F. M., 84
Forbes, T. W., 102
Foster, J. C., 127-128
Fox, G. F., 109
Freud, S.,
  on anal erotism, 14-15
  on cathexis, 38-39
  on dreams, 128-129
  on erotogenesis, 2
  on fixation, 76
  on genital erotism, 15
  on homosexuality, 47, 51
  on infantile amnesia, 106
  on latency period, 45
  on libido theory, 18-19
  on object choice, 38-39
  on Oedipus situation, 38-39, 41, 47
  on paranoia, 71
  on perversion, 62
  on pleasure-sucking, 7
  on projection, 121
  on psychoanalytic process, x
  on regression, 76
  on repression, 105-106
  on sex curiosity, 29
  on sexual overstimulation, 32-33
  on thumbsucking, 4
Frustration, 76
  and regression, 90-98
  removal of reward, 93-94

Gahagan, L., 127
Galbraith, H. M., 50-51
Gardner, G. E., 72-73
Generalization, 87, 91
Goal gradient, 94
Goal object, 77
Guilt feelings,
  and projection, 124-125
  and sexual deviation, 125-126

Halverson, H. M., 3, 8, 15-17, 20-21, 39
Hamilton, G. V., 26-28, 33, 39-40, 43, 46, 47, 48, 49-51, 60-62, 63-64, 67-69, 107
Hamilton, J. A., 85, 90
Harden, L., 108
Harris, W. W., 109

Hattendorf, K. W., 29-30
Healy, W., 122
Heathers, G. L., 89
Heathers, L. B., 115
Henry, G. W., 50-51
Heterosexuality,
  origin of, 43-45
Homosexuality, 34, 47-54, 64, 71-74
  age differences, 47-48
  associative, 51-54
  Hamilton's syndrome, 49-51
  origins of, 49-54
  and paranoia, 71-74
  passive, 52-54, 73
  sex differences, 47-48, 51-52
Honzik, C. H., 82
Horney, K., x
Horton, L. H., 128
Hull, C. L., 94
Humphreys, L. G., 84-85
Huston, P. E., 115-116
Hypersexuality, 32, 62-67
Hypnosis, 98-100, 109, 115-116, 127-128
Hyposexuality, 59-62
Hysteria, 39

Ideas of reference, 74, 122-124
Identification, 52, 55-57, 59
Incestuous feelings, 48
Isaacs, S., 23-25, 28

Jensen, K., 8, 9
Jersild, A. T., 112, 127, 128, 130
Jones, M. R., 14

Kardiner, A., x
Kimmins, C. W., 128, 129-130
Kirkpatrick, C., 54
Klein, D. B., 127-128
Koch, H. L., 15, 17-18, 113
Kopel, D., 127, 131
Krechevsky, I., 82, 85, 90

Landis, C., 31-32, 33-34, 48-49, 51, 62, 64, 110
Latency period, 44, 45-47
Learning theory,
  and psychoanalysis, 35-37, 46-47, 52, 57-58, 76-78, 80-81, 102-103, 136-139
Leeper, R., 112

Levy, D. M., 3-7, 8, 9, 17, 19, 31, 40
Lewin, K., 77, 97-98, 129
Libido,
  components, 19-20
  theory of, 1, 21-22
Linder, R. E., 128, 131-132

Macfarlane, J. W., 4, 9, 19
Malamud, W., 128, 131-132
Malinowski, B., 29, 32, 35-36, 45
Mangus, A. R., 54
Marital partner, 54-55
Markey, F. V., 127, 128, 130
Marriage, 26-27, 31-32, 65
Martin, R. F., 92-93
Masculinity-femininity test, 53-54, 73-74
Masochism, 25, 27, 63, 67-68
  sex differences, 63
Mason, G., 118-119
Masturbation,
  adolescent, 40-41
  genital, 15, 17, 40-41, 49, 50, 61-62, 64
  oral, 7, 22
  sex differences, 17-18, 40
McGranahan, D. V., 116-118
Mead, M., 32, 34-35
Meltzer, H., 112
Menzies, R., 112
Merrill-Palmer clubs, 45
Micturition, 20-21
Middleton, W. C., 127, 128
Miles, C. C., 51-54, 73
Moore, E. H., 112
Mowrer, O. H., 77, 91-92
Murray, H. A., Jr., 121-122

Nailbiting, 9-11
  incidence, 9-10
  measurement of, 9-10
  origins of, 11
Narcissism, 27, 39-40, 50, 63
Nelson, A. K., 3, 7
Neuroticism, 108-109
Nissen, H. W., 84
Nowlis, H. H., 56

Object choice, 38-58
Oedipus influence, 47-49, 131
Oedipus situation, 38-39, 41-45, 61, 136-137

O'Kelly, L. I., 93
Olson, W. C., 10, 11-14
Oral gestures, 11-14
  incidence of, 12
  measurement of, 11-12
  origin of, 12-14
Orgasm inadequacy, 33-34, 59-62, 64, 65-66
  correlates of, 60-62

Pacifiers, 4-5, 19
Page, J., 73-74
Paranoia, 71-74, 124
Parent-child conflict, 42, 43, 50, 66
Parent-child relationship, 41-44
Parent preferences, 42-43
Personality theory, 140-143
Peterson, R. C., 56-57
Petting, 66
Platonow, K. I., 98-99
Pleasure-sucking, 2-8
  incidence of, 4
  independence of motivation, 8
  interference with, 7-8
  as masturbation, 7
  origin of, 3-7
  in puppies, 6-7
Ponderal index, 13
Posner, B. A., 125-126
Postural regression, 102
Pratt, K. C., 3, 7
Prepubertal homoerotism, 47-48
Primitivation of action, 96-98
Projection, 121-126
  experimental induction of, 125-126
  measurement, 124-125
  in paranoia, 71
Projective techniques, 121
Psychoanalysis as theory, ix-x, 133-135
Psychoanalytic method, 133-135, 139-140
Punishment and fixation, 85-86

Reaction formation, 67, 71, 124
Regression, 76-104, 137-139
  constructiveness of play, 96-98
  drive regression, 76
  function of fixation, 92-93, 94-96
  hypnotic, 98-99
  instrumental act regression, 77, 89-96

intelligence, 98-100
object regression, 76
as primitivation, 96-98
with satiation, 94
Reinforcement, 81-83, 84-85, 86
Repression, 32, 47, 71, 105-120
associative, 113-115
by electric shock, 116-118
experimental induction, 115-119
measurement, 110-115
primal, 106
theory, 105-106, 110-111
Retrogression, 77
Riddle, E. E., 109
Rosenzweig, S., 56, 118-119

Sackett, R. S., 89
Sadism, 19, 25, 27, 62, 63, 67-68
sex differences, 63
Sanders, M. J., 90-91
Sanford, R. N., 122
Schizophrenia, 100-102
sleeping postures, 102
thinking, 100-102
Sears, R. R., 69, 74, 77, 106, 110, 115,
116-118, 119, 123-124, 125
Secondary conditioning, 86-87
Secondary drives, 78-81, 86
Self-criticism, 123
Selling, L. S., 130
Sex,
aggressions, 28, 32-35, 49, 60
anxiety, 38-39, 47, 60-62, 71
children's questions, 29-31
curiosity, 25, 28-32
inhibition, 59
neurosis, 32-33
overstimulation, 32-36
perversion, 32-33, 62-67
play, 28-29, 33-34, 45
promiscuity, 50, 65
Sex behavior,
effect of culture, 25-26, 29, 31, 32,
35-37, 43, 46-47, 52, 57-58, 136-137
pathological, 59-75
social development of, 45-46
Sex-consciousness, 46
Sexuality,
genital, 28-37
infantile, 1-2, 38, 135-136
pregenital, 1-15, 18-21, 23-28, 67-70
Shakow, D., 115-116

Sharp, A. A., 113-115
Skinner, B. F., 84
Social-sex maturity scale, 46
Stagner, R., 43, 112-113
Stalnaker, J. M., 109
Stogdill, R. M., 42
Stott, L. H., 43
Strakosch, F. M., 72-73
Sublimation, 67, 70-71
Substitution, x, 22
Success and failure, 55-56, 118-119
Sucking reflex, 2-3
modification of, 7
Sun, K. H., 3, 7
Symonds, P. M., 41

Taylor, W. S., 70-71
Teething, 20
Terman, L. M., 31-32, 33-34, 42, 51-
54, 60-62, 73
Thumbsucking (see Pleasure-sucking)
Thurstone, L. L., 56-57
Time-sample method, 11-14
Topology, regression, 96-98
Traits,
anal, 67-69
projection of, 124-126
Trobriand Islands, culture (see Cul-
ture, Trobriand Islands)
Tumescence, 15-18, 20-21
incidence of, 16
origins of, 16-17, 20-21

Virshup, B., 116-118
Voyeurism, 25, 27, 63
sex differences, 63

Warkentin, J., 73-74
Waters, R. H., 112
Wechsler, D., 9-10
Welch, L., 127
Wells, F. L., 97
White, R. W., 109
Williams, K. A., 78-79
Williams, S. B., 82-83, 87, 88
Willoughby, R. R., 40-41, 47
Witty, P., 127, 131
Wohlgemuth, A., 112
Wolfe, J. B., 79

Young, P. C., 99
Youtz, R. E. P., 82-83, 87, 88